A PARENTS
A R   .. KID

To Emma.

Remember Just
have to watch each
other have ♡

Ashley x

A PARENTS' GUIDE
to raising a

RESILIENT
KID

Ashley Costello

Copyright © 2023 Ashley Costello
Published by Resilient Publishing House

Requests for permission should be sent to
ashley@theresilientkid.co.uk

A CIP catalogue record for this book is available
from the British Library.

Print ISBN: 978-1-7393026-0-3
eBook ISBN: 978-1-7393026-1-0

Edited by Erin Chamberlain
Cover design by Sally Tyson
Internal design by Rebecca Brown
Proofread by Mary Davis

Dedication

To Erin & Finn, the original resilient kids – thank you for showing me how to be your Mummy.

To Dave, there is no one that I would rather walk this parenting journey with.

To Lesley, thank you for being the mum I needed and a fabulous Nin to the kids.

To Jaime, the little sister – thank you for teaching me boundaries and how far I can take a joke.

To the lady writers - you crazy pair - I couldn't have done it without you!

I love you all x

Extra resources

Contents

Introduction

Take a walk with me

As CONTROVERSIAL AS IT SOUNDS, I think there's no such thing as a parenting expert. We are here to guide our kids home, to hold their hands and help get them through this thing we call life.

In my more than twenty years practising as a psychotherapist, I've seen that parenting is hard enough without 'the experts' putting pressure on us. There is already enough pressure from social media – who hasn't seen the perfectly turned-out birthday cakes, or the kids dressed up in matching outfits at Christmas time all over Instagram? And it's all just a snapshot. In reality, the birthday child could be in tears a second after that photo if the birthday cake is cut into the wrong shape or those fancy matching Christmas PJs could be covered with muddy pawprints after the dog photobombed (and knocked the tree flying). Then, there is pressure from schools for kids to perform, to behave and fit in. There is so much that we are trying to navigate as parents.

I support children, adolescents and families with everyday struggles. What I don't do is sit here, barking orders and telling people how they should parent.

After all, despite all my years of experience and quali-fications, my kids still teach me new things every day. Parenting is a journey, and I am here to walk beside you as we navigate this family path.

Why are we here? Why are any of us here? I am not asking you to consider the big question of your personal purpose – or maybe I am! Why am I writing this book for you?

When I was young, my grandparents lived over the road from us, my auntie and cousins lived around the corner, and there were at least another six or seven relatives within a five-mile radius of my house. When I went out with my nanna, we couldn't go five metres without someone saying hello to her or stopping for a conversation. Consequently, everyone who knew her also knew me. That meant if I did something wrong, such as being cheeky, a report of it got back to my nanna and my mum quicker than I could!

It also meant that if I hurt myself, I had people who came out to help within minutes. Now, it wasn't necessarily that I knew everyone who lived near me or that they knew me, but there was always a con-versation above your head about whose kid you were, where you lived, or who you would know. This was safety for a kid, people having your back, keeping you on the straight and narrow – but more importantly, caring about you and what happened to you. Genu-inely caring about how you developed as a child and adolescent and how you turned out as an adult.

We've all heard the old African proverb '**it takes a village to raise a child**'[1] and it is absolutely spot on. But the village that we grew up in just thirty or forty years ago doesn't look anything like the village that our kids are navigating today and relationships are changing because of it. There is a definite correlation between proximity and relationship with the extended family. Families are now often spread out – some all over the world. Today we see kids upstairs in their bedrooms playing games with friends online or scrolling on their phones engaging in a virtual world rather than playing or hanging out with friends. The feeling of community isn't quite as strong – parents are often now working from home, but they do not know or have support from their neighbours and they are living miles from family and the support networks of our childhood – it's no wonder that without our village, we are seeing a corresponding rise in mental health issues in kids[2].

According to latest NHS research, one in six young people, aged 6 to 16, has a mental health problem. Even more concerning, the research shows that one in four 17- to 19-year-olds also have mental health problems. This is currently the same rate as the adults![3] Our kids are missing that wider community connection, the extended family – the aunts and uncles, blood ties or not, who unofficially watch over our kids when we might not be available. Connection is not only the backbone of resilience but it's a basic human need. Research has shown us that loneliness is on the rise and lack of human connection is considered more harmful to our health than obesity or smoking.[4]

Ram Dass, in his book, *Walking Each Other Home* writes:

'We are all in this together, parallel souls on a parallel journey ...'[5]

I will be honest with you: this statement profoundly shook me. As parents we constantly worry. Are doing things wrong? Are we doing good enough? Or worse still, are we damaging our kids? After reading Ram Dass, I thought that is it! Our job as parents, educators, adults in the community, is to simply walk our kids home, the best way we know how.

That said, I am not suggesting we always know best. Sometimes we need advice or support to do this – in the words of Maya Angelou:

'Do the best you can until you know better. Then when you know better, do better.'[6]

That's all any of us want, isn't it? To do better for our kids. I will say **our** kids, **our** children all the way through this, as I fundamentally believe all kids are our responsibility. We must be that village, with the kids we raise, with our friends' kids, with the kids we teach and even those we meet out in our communities.

How to read this book

I'd like to invite you to come on a journey with me through this book. We're going to attempt to put aside all the worries and stresses that brought you to pick up this book and start at the beginning. The format of this book follows four parts.

The first part is this introduction to why I felt compelled to write a guide for parents, as a parent myself and for all you out there. To be honest, it's not just for parents. Speaking to parents first is something that helps identify who the book is for and where you might find it on the shelf of a bookshop or on the virtual shelf of an online retailer. If you work with, volunteer or are simply around kids then this book will help you – and, even if you aren't a parent specifically, you will quickly see in the chapter about connections just how important you are in kids' lives. I'll be referring to you as kids' champions through this book.

Part two, found in chapters one through four, is all the background stuff that makes life navigating kids easier. You might be tempted to skip past this and go straight for the good stuff, but I strongly suggest you don't. This is the cement between those bricks, and it will without a doubt will come into its own when you are in that high stress situation and your kid is shouting at you or inconsolably crying.

In part three, chapter five, Your resilient kid, is the real reason you picked up this book. Because we both want your kids to grow in resilience, this part will start you on the journey of doing this together with the kids in your life. We will explore resilience. What it is, all the components or bricks that make up resilience and how we can boost it for your kids, in an easy and practical way.

Part four is how to do all of the above one step at a time. You will also see conclusions to some of the real life stories that are scattered throughout the book.

You will find action steps in each part of the book but scan the QR code on the next page (or at the front of the book) for many extra resources that you can use every day with your kids, including chore charts, how to host a family meeting and my super successful and heartwarming – how to connect with your teen challenge.

Each chapter can be read in isolation, but I recommend that you read each section in turn as things will start to make sense and build on each other – with the aim of making your parenting and life easier.

You will find all the names of clients or case studies have been changed to those of my beloved nieces and nephews. This is to give privacy to my clients while also giving a nod to my own family village.

Why I help young people

When I was sixteen, my dad woke us all up at midnight and gathered my little sister, my mum and me in the living room. He then told us in a very serious tone that the world was going to end and that we needed to be together. Dad was usually so laid back – he was practically horizontal. He was the one that calmed any situation, he always had a pocketful of dad jokes at the ready, so as you can imagine this was very out of character for him. As a sixteen-year-old this shook my world. I cannot imagine what it did to my mum or my six-year-old sister. My mum did her best to try to calm him, cajole him and argue for us to return to bed. Eventually, we did and, in the morning, he was gone. He was found by his parents at the grave of his grandparents, barefoot, two and half miles away.

My dad had a nervous breakdown, caused by a chemical imbalance through stress. It took hospitalisation and a series of testing medications to rebalance the chemicals for dad to return to his old self. In the meantime, there was no support for us as a family. My sister went to my grandparents on the weekends to take her out of the situation. My mum was left with worry and all the questions. Would he get better? Would he ever be back to his usual jolly self? Would he be able to go back to work? I was old enough to know that mum was worried and felt compelled not to add to that. So, I didn't have anyone really to talk to about what had happened. You don't go to school and say your dad has been taken to hospital because he thinks the world is going to end.

Luckily for us my dad recovered fully and was back to himself within a few months. That day I knew I wanted to be the person that Ashley-the-teen needed at that time. And my journey, learning how to help her, started. I went to university to study psychology and then therapy, with a specialisation in young people. And then I became a teacher. I have worked in various countries around the world, in hundreds of schools and colleges, and with thousands of families. Today I am proud to say I am **the** person that can support kids going through their struggles.

After twenty-five years of experience and a growing community of supporters, whether it's through emails or messages on social media or face to face, my network knows (and you soon will too, if this is the first time you've come across me) that I can help not just their child with their struggles but also them be more confident parents.

How can we be the village our kids need?

Our job, as parents and champions, is to hold our child's hand and walk them through this world with all the feelings, experiences and love we can.

How do we do that?

In my experience, it always starts with emotional regulation. Research highlights the importance of resilience in mental health,[7] whether that be ours as adults or in our kids. Having good mental health is how we handle stress, it is having an understanding of our emotions, being able not just to label them but to express them in a healthy way. We call this emotional regulation. It's how we as parents and keep from blowing our top when things don't go according to plan. For example, we notice milk down their uniform or the dog has been sick in your work bag as you're about to walk out the door for school drop off or you're waiting for that last kid, who's always last to settle down before you start your class lesson.

Then, how do we help them keep a lid on **their** emotions? As parents and champions, we are not always aware, or we don't understand the impact, of our kids' brain development on their emotional development. We walk alongside our babies, watching them learn to walk and talk, getting up to all kinds of mischief. Then our babies get taller and hit puberty – and we think, yay we did it! Job done! They may be grown but our brains do not develop fully until we are late into our twenties. Our kids need us for a long time, helping them walk through and process their emotions. If emotional regulation is of particular interest to you, turn to chapter four where I go into much more detail about it.

For those already thinking, 'I'm not sure I do this very well' or 'this parenting malarkey is too hard' or maybe you are thinking you have already failed your kids, let me tell you some good news. Research states we only need to get this parenting thing right thirty percent of the time for our kids to turn out well. Read that again. **Thirty percent!** This means we can do less than our best seventy percent of the time and they still turn out ok![8]

Real-life example

Emma is a parent to three fabulous kids. She separated from their father when the youngest was still a toddler and brought them up without much help from their dad. Emma would often get to the end of her tether as one or more of the kids would be messing around or misbehaving. 'I always feel like they tag team. When one starts to behave, they tag another one in that starts to act up.' Emma's way of dealing with kids on top of stresses with work and running a house singlehanded is to shout at them. 'I feel like I do all the asking nicely but they don't listen until I begin to shout.' She would then feel enormous guilt for losing her temper with them. 'I would shout at them, then feel guilty about everything, the shouting, the separation from their dad, even what they had for dinner.' When I first met Emma, one of the first things I said to her was, 'How often do you think you get this parenting malarky right?' She replied, 'About 50/50.' I told her about the thirty percent research. The facts are that it's more about showing up for our kids than being perfect. Modelling for them the repair after we lose it. Deepening those connections and building their resilience.

The heart of parenting

This, for me, is the heart of our role – whether we parent, teach, guide, or watch out for them – we are here to walk these kids home and help them regulate and navigate their emotions on the way.

This book has been a long time in coming. I've been dreaming about writing it since before my TEDx talk, before my business, The Resilient Kid. All the thoughts and the practices I've created have been percolating in the back of my mind for years, it almost feels like it's my life's work to contribute to how – and why – we need to build resilience in our kids.

Children who have resilience can bounce back from the challenges that life throws at them. They recover more quickly from trauma and setbacks, allowing them to build their confidence and problem-solving skills on the way. These children are less likely to give up and quit when things get tough.

If our kids don't have the resilience they need, we tend to see them struggling with uncomfortable emotions such as sadness, anxiety, disappointment, frustration, and so on. They don't have the awareness that these emotions are temporary, and all will be ok in the end.

Those children who lack resilience will tend to become aggressive or defensive as they try to deal with challenges in unhealthy ways such as self-harm (everything from banging their head to cutting), following their peers with risky behaviour or isolating themselves away from others.

The fact is children who are resilient have better mental and physical health.[9] This is why it is so important that we build their resilience and future-proof our kids, not just for now but for a time that we are not walking beside them holding their hand and they are alone with all the pressures of negotiating the big wide world.

I hope that whatever capacity you are in as you come to this book, it strikes a chord for you too.

And thank you!

For buying the book, for believing in me but more importantly for wanting to do better for all our kids! Let's get this party started.

Chapter one:
What is resilience?

THE 12TH EDITION OF THE *Oxford English Dictionary* defines resilience as:

'The ability of people or things to withstand or recover quickly from difficult conditions'[10]

I think this definition falls short in many ways, particularly when talking about resilience and kids. The word resilience is bandied about a lot and we need to have a real understanding of what it means when we talk to kids about it. Firstly, it's important to know that resilience is something we can build rather than something we have or we don't have. Resilience is not reserved for special people, such as Olympians – we all have access to it. If we imagine a wall of resilience made up of individual bricks or components, then whatever life throws at us we have that defence ready and standing. To put it another way, if it is raining outside, we would grab an umbrella – we wouldn't go out unprepared. It is the same with resilience. We know that there will be many challenges throughout our lifetime, so why not grab your brolly and protect yourself from the rain? The good news is that as adults in the lives of these kids we can help build the walls with them.

There are eight traits or bricks in the wall of resilience. They are:

- Courage
- Empathy
- Gratitude
- Purpose
- Contribution
- Responsibility
- Self-care and health
- Connection and belonging

These bricks of resilience aren't simply things you either have or you don't have. They are all developed through time, experience and relationships – essentially as we live life. You may well be inherently adept at some of them, but they all require nurturing and developing. This is where you, the parent or champion, come in. We can do seemingly small things that will cultivate resilience, whether it's building our kid's connections with cousins or family friends, giving them small challenges to build confidence, or igniting their purpose with little adventures. We can help build and stabilise their wall by actively looking for the gaps in their resilience and encouraging practical ways to fill them. All of this makes for a stronger wall, a stronger defence in times of stress – a wall of resilience – that you help build. I want to add here that even if **you** don't feel resilient, you can absolutely still build resilience in your kids and you never know, the nice little side effect of building with your kids might be that your own wall of resilience gets built and strengthened too.

Is your kid an Orchid or a Dandelion?

Why do some kids have resilience and some just don't?

We all know those kids who seem to thrive no matter the circumstances and those who are more sensitive and need more support. Why is that?

Dr Thomas Boyce, an American professor of paediatrics, studied environmental, biological and social differences in children. He came up with a theory that there are two types of children.[11]

> **The Dandelion child**
> They are as hardy as the flower –
> healthy, resilient – they can thrive
> under most circumstances and in most
> environments.

> **The Orchid child**
> They appear sensitive, fragile and
> susceptible. These children may struggle
> in challenging environments However,
> given the right support, they can excel.

My two children are a great example of this theory. They have had the same upbringing, the same parents. They have moved houses, hell, they've moved countries together! They have lost grandparents they were close to and started new schools twice. The first one, our Dandelion, is resilient and self-sufficient, academic and will help around the house without being asked. While the other, our Orchid is much more sensitive, gets very emotional when told off by teachers or other adults, is much more empathetic to those around them and although holds their own academically is much more creative. They do, however, have to be strong armed into tidying their room.

Why is it that two kids brought up in the same environment, with the same parents, can be so different?

There are many reasons that kids are different. Their birth order can have an effect – firstborn kids tend to get more undivided attention from parents. Becoming parents, especially immediately after birth, can be difficult. Did the parents struggle physically? This could include how well you recovered after the birth or how well you coped with all the aspects of having a new baby in the house. Did the parents struggle emotionally – was there any support offered? Did the parents struggle to bond or emotionally adjust to the new baby? Even how much support they received from extended family at the time can affect kids and how they interact with the world. The stories they were told about their birth can even have an impact 'you were late', 'you were a difficult baby' or 'you were an ugly baby' all become that internal narrative to 'I'm always late', 'I am difficult' or 'I am ugly' When often it may well be that it was the dates were wrong, it was a difficult birth, or you came out squashed.

Let's go back to Dr Boyce's theory. Orchid children are far more likely to be introverted, sensitive to their environment and can easily be overwhelmed. Dandelion children, however, are more resilient, overcome challenges more easily and appear more outgoing and adaptable. The characteristics match exactly to most people's experiences of the plants they were named after. Do you have that orchid sitting on the kitchen windowsill that was blooming when you received it as a gift but hasn't bloomed since? You've watered it, you bought fancy feed for it, you have religiously tended to it but it ends up looking just like a stick growing out of a pot? Or maybe you have a lawn full of dandelions that no matter what treatment you put on them or how many times you mow them they just keep popping back up? You get the picture. My children are near perfect examples of each of the categories – one can be pretty much left to their own devices and the other needs regular tending.

Dr Boyce's work is groundbreaking in itself but also because it highlights what I see in my everyday practice.

Real-life example

Marcus' parents had split up and were living separately at the time I met the family. One parent had a new partner and their family living with them. Marcus' brother had adjusted well to the arrangement; Marcus had not. His mum reported that he had suddenly had lots of angry outbursts, fussy eating, that he did not want to be separated from her and that he was becoming quite controlling with her and what happened in the house. Both boys had been raised the same way, with the same parents until now, yet one adapted to the new situation while the other didn't. When we look at Dr Boyce's work, we can see in his analogy with the flowers that one always needs more tending than the other. It was no different with Marcus and his brother. Marcus' mum was seeing this as acting out when actually he was saying, 'I need help.' Holistically to help the whole child we had to help those around them too. Reframing Marcus' behaviour with mum, dad and teachers, giving them tools to manage and guide him was my first step in supporting them. Next, I worked with Marcus, helping him to recognise his emotions and giving him strategies to process what was going on for him. We then looked at why he became so attached to his mum and how we could lessen that but still feel secure. Putting these tools together meant Marcus had the support he needed and the tools to get through it. Afterwards his mum said, 'I can't believe the change in me and Marcus ... you have literally changed our lives'.

Dr Boyce's work is so important in relation to resilience. He proves that both types of children can go on to thrive with the right support, no matter how they started off in life and whether they were a hardy dandelion or a sensitive orchid.

How do we know that our children are not resilient?

I met Mary about four years ago. She had three children and she had lived in the same place since they were born, so all of her kids went through the same schools with familiar teachers and friends around them. 'What I don't understand, Ashley, is why my middle one is so sensitive and anxious.' Mary went on to say that her child was very down on themselves, talked negatively about their abilities, their body, and blamed themselves for things going wrong. This is an all too familiar story. If it's not sensitivity, it's the other side of the coin – not taking responsibility and blaming others around them for their mistakes. Every time I speak to a parent about their child, resilience comes up in one way or another without fail. Hell, it comes up that often I named my business after it!

How does low resilience show up in our kids?

Low resilience can show up in many different ways with our kids, which we will look at in more detail below, but in short it is often their response to stress. This is our cue to see what we can do to recognise it and build that resilience.

The Perfectionist – These kids fear failure
- They have unrealistically high expectations of what they can achieve and almost become paralysed and overwhelmed with doing everything perfectly.
- They often don't fulfil their full potential because they worry that they'll not do as well as they'd like.
- They get easily frustrated when getting things wrong, often ending in outbursts of anger or tears. This can lead to them abandoning homework or tasks altogether.
- They may restart a project over and over due to worry that it's not right or perfect.
- Perfectionist kids will often stick to what they know, rather than challenge

themselves with new activities, foods and even making new friends.

- They often miss out on new opportunities. Over time it can limit their confidence and personal growth by avoiding making mistakes. Mistakes and failing at things help us grow as human beings.
- They often become self-conscious and struggle with low self esteem.

Real-life example

Nandi was an amazing artist. She was studying Art at college and had been chosen for an exhibition with her school artwork the year before. She had a good reputation and had been highly recommended. Within three months of starting her new course, she had become anxious, she continually procrastinated with her artwork and her emotional outbursts were affecting the whole family. When I met Nandi and we talked through what was happening for her, she began to recognise the pressure she was putting on herself. She realised that she hadn't finished a piece of art because she was worried that it wouldn't be up to her usual standard. We talk about what Nandi got out of her art, besides her grades. She talked of the freedom of being able to lose herself in it, being able to express her emotions whether she felt in a good or bad mood, the connection to something bigger than herself. The way Nandi talked about her craft was way beyond her years and I could fully understand why she was so good. We also explored her fear of not being good enough and the pressures and expectations she was putting on herself.

We also talked to her parents and teachers about their expectations – which were not as high as her own. Nandi reframed her fear and enjoyed the process of making her art again – whenever she started to feel the pressure of failure looming she would use the strategies we worked on and take a step back. Nandi said, 'I fell back in love with the process, rather than the outcome.'

The Comfort Zoner – These kids don't fear failure, they fear success

- This feeling differs from fear of failure in so much as they worry about other people's view of their success.
- They may not work as hard as they can or they might even stop working, so they can say they didn't try, rather than that they failed to reach their expectations.
- They hate the thought of the extra attention success may bring.
- Kids, usually teens, worry about the isolation from their peers, singling them out to be different than friends or classmates with their success. This can lead to embarrassment – the ultimate social faux pas for teens.
- Often these kids become anxious about being taken down from that lofty position where others might have placed them, whether they wanted to be placed there or not.
- It is similar to fear of failure and the Perfectionist archetype as it can limit their potential in life.

- Procrastination is also a trait of this characteristic – these kids tend to put off what they need to do.
- These kids excel at self-sabotage – often on the verge of success they will come up with reasons to quit.
- Watch out for self-destructive tendencies. Sometimes these kids will turn to unhealthy behaviour to derail their own success.

Real-life example

I often see the Comfort Zoner when I'm working with final year university students. They have completed the earlier stages of their course with flying colours, they have a good group of friends and are looking after themselves and have all that independence entails. As talk of careers and finals emerge, there can be a sudden downturn in their behaviour and motivation. Students will start to sabotage themselves. Henry, a final year student, was on course for a good degree. He had a part-time job, great housemates and a girlfriend. He stopped turning up for work, started turning in uni work late, and drinking more than usual. His teachers and parents were concerned about him. His family got in touch and after a few sessions we unpicked what was going on for Henry. 'I felt like real life was coming crashing towards me, the expectations from everyone around me were big! Would I get a job, a house, settle down with my girlfriend ...? I just didn't feel ready for that kind of responsibility.' Henry's issue wasn't that he couldn't do it but more that he could – and the responsibility and expectations that came with that success weighed him down. We looked at Henry's next steps rather than the bigger picture. I supported Henry to talk to his parents about how he felt and how they could support him. Working on his motivation and priorities one step at a time, Henry left university with a really good degree.

The Critic – These kids talk about themselves negatively

- Everyone has that inner voice that may be occasionally critical, but if it keeps saying bad things, that can have a damaging effect on their self-esteem.
- Often kids talk negatively about their abilities, 'I'm no good at maths, art, languages ...' This is often seen around school subjects where the culture is whether you are either good at them or not.
- Negative self-criticism can be seen in lots of things such as friendships. 'They don't like me' or 'I'm a rubbish friend.'
- One of the most popular negative self-talk topics is about their bodies. 'I'm ugly, fat, too short ...'
- All of these voices can be a way of protecting themselves from social pressure – saying it before a peer or bully does.
- Sometimes kids speak negatively out loud because they need reassurance from adults in their lives. For example, the adult will say, 'You're not fat' or 'You are good at maths' when they hear the critical comments. We all need reassurance every now and then.

- Look for globalised thinking. When these Critic kids don't do well in one thing it becomes all or nothing thinking. For example, 'I'm rubbish at netball' when they only lost one game. It can really chip away at their self-esteem and confidence to try new experiences.

Real-life example

A few years ago, I had a student who loved art, in every sense of the word. She was creative and enjoyed various mediums. She created a self-portrait and a teacher 'corrected' the eyes for her. From that day on this child thought she was not good at art and quickly switched her interests elsewhere. As adults we often see it from our point of view. We think 'let's make it the best, let's put it on display', when what the child often takes away from this sort of feedback is 'I'm not good enough.' Nothing was ever said overtly about their artistic abilities and I am sure the teacher would be upset to think they had had that effect on their student. However this then becomes that critical internal voice.

The Projector – These kids blame others

- They blame others – teachers, siblings, parents, friends – for things going wrong.
- It is a sign they don't have the confidence or self-esteem to take responsibility.
- Sometimes it's because they don't want to feel shame. It is easier to deny or blame others than to admit mistakes.

- It can be because they want to be seen as the expert and don't want to be embarrassed that they don't know.
- They often don't want to disappoint the adults around them.
- Often they don't have the capacity to manage their feelings, so will either ignore or blame those around them.

Real-life example

Melvin was a card shark. I can't remember how many different ways he skilfully cheated his way to victory. You might wonder what that has to do with blaming others? However, it is very indicative of not wanting to lose face, not being in the wrong or wanting to be seen as the expert. Melvin was a great little guy but he would often blame everyone around him for things that happened from not understanding his homework (teachers' fault for not explaining it) to spilling juice down his top (mum's fault for distracting him).

The Conservative – These kids are resistant to change

- They shy away from trying new things, it doesn't matter if it is new foods, new activities or even making new friends.
- Children like this that are less adventurous often struggle with their confidence.
- They don't want to fail, or they don't know what is expected of them, so the safer option is to stick with what they know.
- This trait limits their life experiences and opportunities to build confidence.

- Their inflexibility can cause issues in the wider family, for example, wanting to sit in a certain place or use a certain cup.
- Transitions also tend to be difficult for the Conservative kid.
- They can react disproportionately to a situation, having unexplained meltdowns.

Real-life example

Lilia had struggled with the separation of her parents and began to rigidly stick to her routines. She began to dictate where things went in the house, who sat where and when everyone ate – much to parents' and other siblings' annoyance. Working with Lilia and her family, I gave her tools to express her emotions in a safe and controlled way, worked with mum and dad to prepare Lilia for changes and make small steps to her feeling comfortable and safe with change and transitions.

The Worrier – These kids worry excessively

- Kids often worry about all sorts of things, many of which are out of their control – for example, wars around the world and climate change.
- They also worry about the everyday things, such as will they get collected from school (despite you never forgetting to get them) or what if they get asked to read aloud in class.
- Anxiety is like a runaway train once it starts around one thing – it can very easily transfer to other things in kids if they are not given the tools to manage it.

- Once children and adults have the strategies to manage anxiety, their resilience improves.
- Resilience is an antidote to worrying excessively.

Real-life example

Jay's family came to me when they noticed Jay seemed to be worrying excessively, often about seemingly small things. Jay was worrying about being collected after school by their mum. Jay had never been forgotten, but this worry then began to permeate other areas of their life. When I worked with Jay, they told me of their Grandmother's death not long before our meeting. They told me all about their need to know who was collecting and when. When we unpacked all the feelings, it became clear that Jay was worried that something may happen to their mum or dad. We talked lots about Grandma and worked through Jay's grief and anxiety around losing their parents. We then made a plan with mum and dad to ease Jay's worry about being left.

The Sensitive – These kids are sensitive to their surroundings

- They often burst into tears for no apparent reason.
- They are the typical Orchid children from Dr Boyce's research.
- They often feel overwhelmed and don't have the tools to process or manage their emotions.
- They often ask lots of questions and need lots of reassurance.

- They get overwhelmed easily by noise, sometimes even by smells or lights.
- Emotional regulation is a key foundation to building resilience in Sensitive kids.
- They can be picky eaters.
- They may struggle with transitions.

Real-life example

Noah was struggling when his family came to me. His older brother has been happy-go-lucky, so Noah's mums didn't know what to do this time around. Noah would often cry over what seemed like the smallest thing. He would worry a lot, especially over changes, and get easily overwhelmed when they were on days out. If any adult shouted or just raised their voice that would really upset Noah and he would dwell on it for days. My job started with the parents – it became clear when chatting to the mums that they both had very different ways of disciplining the boys. What was working with the older brother wasn't working with Noah. We looked at a more gentle approach with natural consequences rather than punishment. We built in lots of emotional support ahead of transitions or change in the house and looked at Noah's own boundaries and needs. 'He's like a different little lad. He has just blossomed. He occasionally bursts into tears but usually we can recognise his needs ahead of time.'

Acknowledging a sensitive child and their needs and giving them the tools to be able to freely express themselves is key – only then can they begin to build resilience.

As adults, if we examine our own life, we can see the examples above playing out. We also might give up on a task or not take an opportunity through the fear of failing or lack of confidence. We keep to the same old routines because that is safer and helps to keep our anxiety at bay rather than taking on that new role at work or challenge in our personal life. Is this what we want for our kids? Do we want our kids to play it safe, or do we want them to take healthy risks and have the tools to recover well when they are stressed or things don't go according to plan? My guess is, as parents and kids' champions, we want to give them all the tools and guide them in building that wall of resilience.

Chapter two:
Brain development and resilience

LET'S GO BEHIND THE SCENES and look at the neuroscience behind resilience. At this moment you might say, 'What's the brain got to do with it anyway, Ashley?' Well, in short, EVERYTHING!

We have all been there, in the supermarket or coffee shop, and a kid is having a meltdown. Part of you at this point is saying a silent prayer of thanks that it's not your kid and the other smug part of you is judging that kid and probably that parent. Until it's your turn and you remember very quickly what it's like to have a kid acting out – oh the shame! I'm here to tell you no one is to blame in these situations and there certainly should be no shame, only empathy for all involved. What we often don't realise is that when kids have a meltdown, they are not in contact with the parts of the brain that can help them calm down or see things rationally.

We are the only species on the planet who can study its own brain (known as mindsight) so we are uniquely placed to be able to understand why we respond or react in various ways. Dr Dan Siegel describes the brain using the model of a hand as an illustration.[12]

Action: Make a fist, with your thumb inside and your fingers curled over the top

If you take your hand and think of your wrist as the spinal cord (communication highway), the brain sits on top, your thumb is your **amygdala** the area responsible for the 'instantaneous survival response' (otherwise known as fight, flight or freeze).

Now curl your fingers over the top of your thumb and you will have your **prefrontal cortex**, which is where our rational decision-making processes take place.

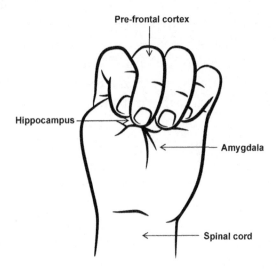

When we are calm, all these areas are nicely connected. If something happens, we can respond easily and appropriately. However, if our fight, flight or freeze centre is triggered then we 'flip our lid'. Lift

your fingers up to see the physical disconnection of the prefrontal cortex.

Being from Manchester originally, I thought this was a term that only we used but no, Dr Dan has popularised it to mean the same in the scientific community too. When we **'flip our lid'** (as we would say in Manchester on a Saturday night in the kebab shop) we lose the ability to communicate effectively with the rational part of our brain and we lose the control over our emotions. Simply put, the upstairs part of the brain, the prefrontal cortex – the part that problem solves, creates and analyses – has disconnected from the downstairs part of the brain, the amygdala – the fight, flight or freeze part – that has detected a threatening situation. When these are disconnected, adults or children struggle to control their emotions or respond to reasoning.

Real-life example

Imagine you're driving your car and another driver cuts in front of you from out of nowhere. Your amygdala will perceive that as a threat. Cortisol, the stress hormone, will be released around the body to get your heart racing in readiness to fight, take flight or freeze. Your hippocampus will have memories and experiences stored and linked to emotions and you will use these to respond accordingly. Your response could vary depending on previous experiences. It could be that you get out of their sight as fast as you can (flight). You might pull over and be overcome with emotions, maybe even shaking physically (freeze). Or maybe you give them a hand gesture and go racing after them, in a furious rage (fight).

Real-life example

Sam has just fallen over in the playground. He isn't hurt too much so jumps up, hopefully before anyone sees him. Then a friend laughs and, out of pure embarrassment, Sam does one of three things: runs away (flight), bursts out crying (freeze), or pushes or punches the friend (fight).

So now you can see why it's so important that we understand how the brain works if we are to guide our young people in how to manage their emotions.

I previously held a position as a therapist for an 1,800-pupil school in Abu Dhabi. One of my projects was to establish emotional regulation lessons. I taught the hand model of the brain to the three-year-olds and above. We talked about the amygdala being the guard dog, the hippocampus being a memory box and the prefrontal cortex being the wise old owl. Now I have to be honest, the school principal was from a physics background and didn't hold therapy in high regard, but over there you can't open a school without a counsellor in residence and, boy, did I use this to my advantage! Within six weeks, the three-year-olds were using the correct terms for parts of the brain, their behaviour had improved, and they were able to express their emotions more easily. Parents were reporting that behaviour and general mood was improved at home too. This was obviously music to my ears but the icing on the cake? When the principal walked past a classroom and heard the little ones saying, when discussing why Tommy had ripped up his sheet of paper, 'Miss, that's because his prefrontal cortex wasn't in charge!' Not because that was a feather in my cap but more because the principal realised the kids knew what they were talking about and could see it in practice.

Is this for real?

Our brains don't know the difference between what is real and what is imaginary. In real life, this means that if we imagine a stressful situation our brain produces adrenaline and cortisol (stress hormones) just as though we are in the middle of that situation. This means that anytime there is a 'perceived threat' our amygdala is triggered.

Real-life example

When we are watching a scary movie, we jump out of our skin even though the action is just on the screen. Our brain sees what is happening in the scene as a real threat – our hearts start pumping, muscles tense, and our breathing might even change. We respond in exactly the same way we would for a real-life experience.

The issue here is that our amygdala is almost constantly triggering our nervous system with perceived imaginary threats and not just priming us to escape from a truly dangerous situation. These triggers could be:

Embarrassment. Remember Sam, who fell over in the playground (see page 32). But also remember our teens, who can get very embarrassed, especially if pride is at stake. A stress response can be triggered by anything from getting a question wrong to what their parents are wearing.

Fright. Something or someone has scared a child. A stress response could be triggered by a shouting adult, a new maths challenge or a stranger in the classroom. All of these can be perceived as a threat, even if an adult is shouting to keep that child safe: 'Watch out for that car!'

Stress. Children and teens can feel stress at seen and unseen threats such as exams, academic or peer pressure, family issues such as death, divorce or financial worries (lots of children talk to me about money worries, whether they have heard parents talk about their worries or if they hear it on the news). All of these examples can trigger the physical symptoms of flight, fight or freeze.

Hungry or hangry. This is a big one in our house and it's important to look at basic needs when kids start to have that all too familiar meltdown. Are they tired, hungry or thirsty? Have they eaten breakfast before school? What did they eat? Sometimes this can have an impact. For example, has the child eaten sugary cereal early in the morning? This can lead to a sugar crash, which the body perceives as a threat. I have seen this in hundreds of classrooms. After morning catch-ups and the class register is done, everything is fine and peaceful, then the first lesson or challenge of the day is presented by the teacher and the seemingly happy-go-lucky student flips their lid. In the classroom this behaviour might look like defiance, anger or picking a fight with someone (fight). There could be an emotional outburst, such as crying or saying they can't do it (freeze). Or what often goes undetected is flight – where the kid shuts down, doesn't ask for help, does not understand what is expected of them and often goes under the radar of the adults in the room, which if reoccurring, could lead to them falling behind. All this from sugary cereal!

Thirst. Also watch out for dehydration. Research has shown[13] that a student's cognitive performance is severely impacted when they don't have enough water. In other words, kids need constant access to clean water (nothing added) to help their brain function better and, more importantly for the classroom, to learn. We need to encourage everyone to drink more water and make sure students have access to water bottles on their desks. It will not only help settle their fight and flight response if they are drinking throughout the day – but also acts as a signal to the brain that they are safe.

Temperature. If we get too hot or too cold (especially if we are trying to learn) this is a perceived threat to the brain and the body. The body then begins to work overtime to regulate our temperature. Think about kids playing outside at lunch, running around and getting hot. They take their jumpers off. Then break is over and they come back into a classroom, which might be cold. The teacher then challenges them with a new piece of work – before they have even thought about putting their jumper back on. They become cold, and without understanding why, become overwhelmed and are more susceptible to flipping their lids. Kids don't always reach for their jumper when temperatures change in the body quickly, it's up to us adults to keep our eyes out for the basic needs.

Worry. A kid can be worried about something without us realising but then, when we ask something of them, they become overwhelmed and flip their lid. For example, your kid may be excited about staying over at a friend's house but worried about the food they will be offered there. Will they like it? Do they have to eat it all? Will they be seen as rude? Will they be hungry? It may seem like a small concern to us as adults, but this is a perceived threat for the brain and can see unexpected and often unexplained behaviour in our kids.

These are some of the many reasons a child can 'flip their lid' (which anyone who has served a toddler triangle toast instead of square can attest to) which can have nothing to do with the actual issue faced. As parents, our job is to understand and spot the 'triggers' to help us deal with the situations or, better still, prevent them from happening in the first place.

It takes how long for our kids to calm down?

When our kids (or when we) flip our lids, responses can be seen in a variety of ways and can take longer than you think to return to the natural resting state where they no longer feel threatened. What happens physically when we feel under threat?

Breathing and heart rate increase. This allows the body to send more oxygen to the blood where it is needed, especially to the brain, but this can cause a rise in blood pressure.

Looks pale or flushed. This is because the blood goes to key areas around the body, especially the internal organs.

Muscles tense. The body prepares to run or fight. This can show up as shaking, but this physical response can also cause your throat to constrict, your voice to become higher pitched and your mouth to become dry.

Pupils become dilated. This sounds strange but it actually allows you to see your surroundings better, which helps us see potential threats.

Physically freeze. Some people freeze, which seems to give the brain more time to scan and find the best response. They can continue to scan the environment while motionless.

Physically flop. Some people flop down, which seems to work in two ways – the threat thinks you're dead (in the situation of being chased) so hopefully will leave you alone (you've probably seen this in movies) or often this works as a dissociation from what is happening. We see this in our kids when they zone out or, in extremes, faint.

Fawn. This physical response is not often mentioned alongside fight, flight or freeze. This is often a direct response to childhood trauma. Kids often go into people pleasing mode, trying to appease the person they feel threatened by.

Recovery from fight, flight, freeze

An adult can take twenty to thirty minutes for the body to return to normal after their fight, flight or freeze response has been activated. For kids it generally takes around forty to sixty minutes. They might feel tired, anxious or agitated for longer. We need to be aware of the physical impact switching into this state has on them. Encourage your kids to:

Eat. As soon as possible, even if it's just a snack to ground them back into their body, reassuring the response system that they are safe.

Drink plenty of water. The body has just worked hard, even if your kid didn't physically go anywhere.

Space. Give them some space from others, as embarrassment can be another trigger – often teens and kids don't like to lose face.

Exercise. Get some exercise to dilute the stress hormones – walking or stretching can really help with this. Alternatively, if they are young or at home, a bath can help remove the stress hormones running round the body.

Sleep. On days when kids have flipped their lid, be aware the body will be physically exhausted, so an earlier bedtime can be handy.

Connect. You know your child best – do they want physical contact, such as a hug or cuddle, or do they like to keep their distance? Either way, try to connect as soon as they are ready. Research has shown that physical contact and connection releases oxytocin, the love hormone, calming their nervous system, reducing discomfort and even pain that the person is feeling.[14]

Why 'calm down' never works

As humans our brains see potential threats everywhere. They might not even be real but that doesn't stop us reacting with a fight, flight or freeze response. It is also important for adults to remember that when kids have flipped their lid there is little point in trying to have a rational conversation straight away. We know they need to calm down, but we need to help them regulate their emotions first, so their upstairs brain, or their problem-solving parts, are re-engaged – then we can walk through what just happened. Just like when we are cut up while driving and that red mist descends and there is no talking to us, it's the same for kids. So, what can we do?

Dr Dan Siegel suggests that we:

1. **Connect with the child.** It can be through a hug, eye contact or even just a touch on the arm.
2. **Name it to frame it.** Name the emotion it appears the child is going through. 'It looks like you are *worried* about going back to school in case your friends don't talk to you?'
3. **Model.** Taking these steps models emotional regulation for the child. As they name the emotions, the flipped lid begins to be put back on.

Take charge moment!

There always comes a point when we must take charge as an adult. It might be when safety is involved, you might have a bunch of kids in a classroom, or you might be taking one of your kids out with a group of friends and it happens. Know that now is not the time to attempt to teach them emotional regulation! Take charge of the situation quickly with commands to keep everyone safe. Once done, and everyone is calm, you can then start to address the issues.

Chapter three:
Is behaviour or behaviourism the problem?

BEHAVIOUR IS THE WAY WE act or interact with others. Behaviourism is a psychological therapy that studies behaviour in response to a trigger or stimulus. This trigger could be another person or something in the environment. An example of this would be giving a student a treat for passing a test. The behaviour would be studying hard, the trigger for that behaviour is a promise of reward at the end.

Let's have a look at behaviour. We know that when a child has flipped their lid, there is no reasoning with them about what has just occurred. Often, kids will tell us lies at this point. They may not really mean to lie to us, but their brain is running around trying to get you an answer and is not connected to the part that stores past experiences or even connected to the rational decision-making process parts of the brain. Does that mean that we don't follow through with consequences for unacceptable behaviour, for example speaking disrespectfully or hitting out at a sibling? Absolutely not, just pick a time when they can actually hear you and what you are saying.

The Skinner box experiment

Our education system and lots of parenting techniques are based on the work of B F Skinner, a leading Harvard professor. He believed that behaviour was motivated by consequences and learnt behaviour. He conducted an experiment where a rat was put in a box and was rewarded with food or punished with an electric shock for engaging in certain behaviours, such as lever pressing.[15] This experiment was done in the 1930s and it is what we still base most of our classroom management on now!

Real-life example

In the classroom we often reward good behaviour with house points, sticker charts or treats at the end of the week. When kids do something wrong then we punish them by taking all the points or treats away – or worse, give them detention. I canvassed a local high school and on average they have five percent of their kids in after-school detention a week (not including lunchtime detentions) and over fifty percent of them are repeat offenders. School principals think they will get kids to fall in line but that's simply not the case – kids end up not caring whether they get detention or not. This is all shaping the way they behave.

There are a few things that are out of sync for me with this.

1. When kids flip their lid, they can't make a 'right or good' choice. They don't have access to that part of their brain. So at the time kids are acting out or misbehaving they are not in full control due to their brains not being fully developed yet. Detention is a punishment that could send kids back into fight and flight that got them into trouble in the first place. Again, detentions don't help teach them to regulate their emotions or behave any better. The kids that are usually in detention are usually the ones with low resilience, less likely to be able to manage their emotions and more sensitive to criticism.

2. If kids are encouraged to learn by rewards, there is no internal motivation to want to learn, so what happens when they're off at a job or university, and we must break the news that they don't get stickers anymore?!

3. Isolation punishments can lead to embarrassment or shame for those kids who can't keep a lid on it, and we all know what that leads to – lack of worthiness, which can lead to lower self-esteem and self-belief. Most kids I see who display aggressive behaviours have low self-worth. Isolating them away is not meeting their needs, when ultimately they need to be seen and heard. If we can't address their needs at school,

what chance have they got in work or future relationships?

4. There is an extra bit of research that we don't consider when we think about behaviour management and that's the rat! In the experiment we think about the scientist manipulating the behaviour of the rat – but what if it's the other way round?

Who's controlling who?

'It's like the little rat in the Skinner box who says, "I've got this psychologist under my control. Every time I press the bar, he gives me a food pellet."' – Jess Lair[16]

The entire basis of the outdated research into behaviourism is based on control. I began this book talking about the idea of 'walking each other home' and that is exactly what I think we, as adults, are here to do. I have worked with thousands of kids over the years and did I see my job as trying to control them? Hell, no! I want them to see themselves for who they are – not the behaviour they might display. If we return to the idea of detention for a moment, what if that frequent flyer student, who always gets detention, uses the system to get the connection they desperately need? For me, first and foremost, it is about connection. It is about acknowledging them. After all, don't we all want to be **seen and heard**? That's a big part of what makes us human. Often, kids who are acting out, having a meltdown or whatever you want to call it, are simply asking for help.

Dr Jody Carrington talks about **connection seeking** rather than attention seeking. It is up to us as the adults to connect with the kids in our care, to see past their behaviour to what they need and then teach them how to express that need in an appropriate way.

Making that connection will make a world of difference to their behaviour. Contrary to widely-held belief, kids do want to behave. Have you noticed how kids will play up for some people and not for others? In the classroom setting, research suggested that saying good morning and greeting pupils outside the classroom door improved engagement and classroom disruption decreased. Connecting with them at the end of a long day at school will really help them regulate and process their day and their emotions.[17]

At home, I try to be there for the half an hour straight after the kids return home. Now I know this is not always possible, but I have been able to make it work more now they are a little older. They have a snack and a drink and then talk about 'what's the chat' at school. The snack is important too. It tells their brain they are safe, especially if they haven't had a good day or are concerned about something.

They will tell me everything (well most things) from what they had for lunch, or friendship issues, to someone getting in trouble in class. This is a great time to connect back in with them and show them we are interested. Food is an amazing tool to regulate kids. The right kind of snack helps the brain to release neurotransmitters and hormones that promote emotional health, which helps them to think more clearly and rationally. If I was head of education, I would start every registration in the morning with a healthy snack. This isn't for the kids that haven't eaten for whatever reason, it's to improve focus, problem solving and put kids in the right headspace to learn.

There are two principles at play here:

1. If we are walking them through situations, then we are metaphorically holding their hand through a situation, then this is helping them regulate their emotions and allowing them to problem solve with us, while they feel safe.
2. Let's remember the brain doesn't know the difference between the real and imaginary, which means we can walk through someone else's struggle and that will help wire their brain for future issues that might come up for them – future-proofing our kids. After all, that's how metaphors and stories have worked for thousands of years.

Chapter four:
How do we help our kids regulate their emotions?

OVER MY YEARS OF EXPERIENCE working with all types of kids, I've come to understand that it's not sanctions and rewards that help kids regulate their emotions but boundaries. It's normal and natural for kids to flip their lids – their brains are still developing and will continue to do so well into their twenties – but they need boundaries to help them manage and understand their emotions. This could look like 'it's ok to be angry, it's not ok to hit out.' They internalise this kind of boundary when they are young. If we don't model this, whether it is verbally or physically, how can our kids learn where that line is for them? Are they still hitting out when they are fifteen or twenty-five, when they become too big for us to handle?

How good are boundaries anyway?

Boundaries and routine around the home and school create a feeling of safety and predictability for kids, which then reduces the fear of uncertainty and potential threats. We have seen a lot of uncertainty in the lives of our young people over the last few years and consequently a huge rise in anxiety for them too.

Having routines around meals, bedtimes and lessons all help children to feel safe and secure. They may not like them, but the regularity keeps anxiety at bay. It also teaches them:

Responsibility. Knowing they are in control of their own behaviour and having responsibility for chores feeds a fundamental need that they belong. They are fully part of this family, the class, the unit. It is also part of setting them up for later life; they learn to be responsible for their behaviour and ultimately their own life and the choices they make. Allowing our kids to have choices in life is really important. If they practise smaller choices at home or in the classroom, it allows them more confidence with the larger choices later on in life.

Consequences. These are the best friend of responsibility and are very significant. Punishments don't often work; they usually lead to a child learning to hide their behaviour and working to not to get caught rather than making a positive change. However, natural consequences like going out without a coat or forgetting a PE kit wires the brain to be more likely to remember the coat or the kit for next time. Our memories often attach themselves to triggers, such as cold or having to explain ourselves to the PE teacher.

Real-life example

Kim forgets her PE kit. She rings home and we run to school with it. In her brain the trigger is then set up to ring home. If we don't run to school with the kit (as hard as it is to watch her 'fail') and Kim has to face the consequence of having to borrow a spare or getting in trouble from a teacher, the brain then makes a new neural pathway set to remember and the trigger is set to remember the kit next time. When we jump to the rescue, we rob them of the opportunity to learn and to be responsible but worst of all, we set them up to fail in the future.

Respect. Parents often complain to me that their kids don't respect them and the first question I ask is, 'How often do you say no?' They often don't see the connection straight away. When we say no to a later bedtime, more chocolate, a later curfew or more screen time we are not just doing it for our kids' health but also teaching them about respect and boundaries. Not just respect for us, although it is a great side effect, but respect for the rules in school, other people's boundaries and even the law.

For me it also teaches them that it's ok to say no to others and have a sense of self. It is easy to under-estimate boundaries but, in effect, when we put in a boundary, we are teaching others how we want to be treated. For kids and teens, this means that they have the self-assurance to implement boundaries they feel comfortable with. Think about the kind of issues that might arise as they grow. Friendships? Money? Sex? Or even drugs? When a peer pushes their boundaries, and they say no, if they have grown up with the pattern of 'no could mean yes later down the line', then they struggle to keep to that no. Can you see how important it is that we not only say NO but that we also stick to it?

Saying no is future-proofing our kids.

We are here walking them through this to encourage the feelings (disappointment, anger they can't do what they have asked) and give them space to manage their emotions (or better still walk them through why you said no). Boundaries and routines not only help kids feel safe (and less anxious) but they teach them how they can identify their own needs in life and how to get them met in a positive way. Even as adults sometimes we struggle with that concept.

Emotional regulation

Emotional regulation is taking a step to control the intensity of an emotional experience, whether it's anger or sadness. When we build the skills to regulate our emotions then we no longer have to suppress or avoid them. Emotional regulation is something we can learn, and it can have a positive impact on our physical and mental health as well as the relationships around us.

Our job is to regulate their emotions by walking them through what's happening, as we are the ones with the developed brains (prefrontal cortex to be precise)!

But first.

We need to regulate ourselves.

How do we regulate ourselves?

There are plenty of times that kids do things that send us over the edge. This can happen for two reasons: Firstly, it could be something from our childhood, triggering our own fight and flight, like being ignored. Maybe we feel like we weren't listened to as a child, and being ignored by your kids can bring up those old feelings. Secondly, we can be triggered because we think that our kids' behaviour (like having a meltdown in the supermarket) is a reflection of our parenting skills. For the former, we need to work through these. I get a lot of adults coming to me for this kind of therapy, helping them deal with childhood issues and enabling them to be there more for their own children. The latter trigger is usually resolved by confidence. The more confident we are in our parenting the less likely we are to be triggered by our kids' behaviour.

Real-life example

Reuben has been asked several times to clean his room; he does it quickly so he can return to his games console. Dad has shown him the things he has missed – clothes down the side of the bed and lots of shoes under the desk, etc. Reuben runs downstairs and logs back on, when Dad casually checks the room and begins to lose it. 'I have asked you three times to do this – why are there still clothes by the bed and shoes all over the floor? Is it because you are not listening to me? Or is it because you can't be bothered?' Reuben's dad was one of many who never felt listened to at home. When Reuben ignores his dad, that brings up those childhood wounds and dad ends up flipping his lid.

When kids don't respond how we expect them to and begin shouting, hitting out or ignoring us, it can easily throw up a memory from the way we were parented. We can end up snapping or shouting because we don't feel heard or because we don't know how to deal with those big emotions being displayed. It could be that we feel the need to be right, as we were never given that voice as a child. Your child displaying emotions will spark something in you. It could be positive – they say 'I love you' and you're filled with that lovely warm feeling. Or the opposite, when they shout 'I hate you' from the top of the stairs and you are filled with rage. Either way your brain will respond – whether you respond positively or negatively doesn't just depend on how you were parented but how well you process those emotions.

Real-life example

Lesley was a parent of three, she worked part time, had a supportive husband and loved her kids. However, when it came to her kids not doing as she asked, she would lose it! Usually a calm person, she couldn't understand why this sent her over the edge. She felt tremendous guilt after shouting and would overcompensate for it. The kids would end up shouting back or her husband would step in. The upshot was that the kids didn't do as they were told, and Lesley was left feeling like a failure. Lesley reached out to me to get the kids to listen. I nearly always have a session with the parent first, to get a bit of background and really try to understand the issue before even seeing the kids. I started with a session with Lesley, who was open to talking about it.

When I asked how she felt as a child, the story began to unfold. She said she was brought up in a loving household but there was an attitude of being seen and not heard. She felt growing up that her opinion didn't matter, and she was never really listened to. I asked her, 'How does it feel when the kids ignore you or don't do as they are told?' She said, 'It's the same, I don't feel heard or valued.' The kids, unbeknown to them, were triggering something that Lesley had struggled with growing up. It had triggered her into fight or flight – and she came out shouting. We talked it through over a couple of sessions, coming up with tools Lesley could use with the kids, including giving herself permission to take some time out if she needed. She also explained to the kids the importance of her being heard. Sometimes we must heal the little person inside of us before we parent our kids. But that's a whole other book! For now, though, if this is something that you can immediately see that you struggle with and would like some support on how to build your own emotional resilience toolkit, take a look at my website (www.theresilientkid.co.uk) and particularly at the therapy section or look at the Resilient Kid course (www.theresilientacademy.co.uk/parents-course)

Seven ways to regulate our own emotions

1. **Identify** what is happening to trigger an emotional outburst. As you can see from Lesley's story, it's not always obvious and might require some digging. Once you start to look at the pattern and become more aware, it won't happen as often.

2. **Notice** what is happening in your body. Often there are physical signs that we feel under threat or vulnerable, such as a racing heart, clenching our fists or teeth, or sweating. Tune into what part of your body physically reacts when you become overwhelmed with emotion.

3. **Name what you feel.** This not only improves our emotional literacy but also helps us to identify the emotion more quickly next time. Is it anger, resentment or fear? Naming it also helps us to be able to share with others why we are reacting the way we are. It's great role modelling for kids too.

4. **Take yourself out of the situation.** Tell the kids that you need five minutes. 'I am really angry right now, so I am going to calm down and then we can chat.' This way we are more likely to be able to choose how to respond, rather than responding in the fight or flight reaction we get caught up in.

5. The quickest (and most underrated way) of calming the fight or flight response is to **take big deep breaths** in through the nose and out through the mouth. This helps to regulate and calm the amygdala (our fight or flight centre).

6. **Be kind to yourself.** Berating yourself after you have lost your cool is not going to make you feel any better, or anyone else. Always make amends if you have upset others (another good role modelling lesson for kids) but equally give yourself some praise if you have kept your cool or know that you are at least trying.

7. **Take up exercise.** It really helps with emotional regulation. If we get angry or upset on a regular basis, then those stress hormones sit in our body with nowhere to go. If we move our bodies, whether it is walking, practising yoga or hitting the gym, those nasty hormones will move out and help you regulate emotions easier.

We often feel this enormous pressure to get parenting right but we don't have to get it right all the time. Often, until we look at our triggers, it is hard to know what will set us off until it does. In The Resilient Kid Parents Course, we identify what sends us off in a tailspin.

Real-life example

One parent, Alicia, discovered, 'I couldn't understand why, as a usually calm and rational person, I turned into a raving banshee when the kids disobeyed me. I realised that when I was younger, I was belittled when I didn't obey my dad, he would often shame me and make out like I was too stupid to understand. When I explored my feelings around this, I understood that it wasn't because I wanted to shame my kids, rather I felt protective towards them. I didn't want to experience that same shame I did. Even just the language I used, 'obey', changed. When I realised I wasn't responsible for who they are and just allowed them to be themselves, walking beside them, it wasn't personal, I stopped the shouting and was just there for them, helping them process their feelings.'

How do kids regulate their emotions?

If you thought that emotional regulation stops for our kids as they hit the teens, then think again. In fact, it doesn't usually stop until they are in their early twenties for girls, at around twenty-four, and for boys, at around twenty-seven or twenty-eight years of age. Their brain doesn't stop developing until then, so they will look to us for support or help with regulating their emotions. And let's be honest, emotional regulation, that walking through how we feel, always feels better with someone beside us no matter how old we are.

So how do we help them?

1. **Pick your battles.** Is it so important that your kids eat every bit of broccoli? No, not usually – in fact mealtimes are the one place I say don't battle it out. Kids usually eat when they are hungry. Does it mean they get dessert if they don't eat the majority of the dinner? No. But the more control we want over what they eat, the more they want to gain that control back.

2. **Pick your timing.** If one of your kids is in the middle of a call with friends or playing a game, give them some warning that you need them to come off. Expecting them to respond to your request immediately is unfair. This is particularly true if kids are gaming. If they are playing a competitive game, chances are they are in a fight or flight state, so give them some time to come down from that state before wanting them to engage with you.

3. **Check their basic needs.** If they are having a meltdown, check their basic needs first. Are they hungry, thirsty or tired? There is a ten-year gap between me and my younger sister and when I got in from school as a grumpy teen she used to shout, 'Give that kid a donut!' It became a standing joke, she was five-years-old and could recognise a hangry episode a mile off. (I rarely got a donut, by the way, I think it was wishful thinking on her behalf.) After checking their basic needs, check in with them – have they had a hard day at school or a fall out with friends? Then move on to helping them regulate.

4. **Get close.** If they are small and they will let you pick them up, get them close to you. They will innately physically respond to your nervous system. If you are nice and calm, they will follow suit. I remember my eldest being in the pushchair in a busy shopping mall. She was about two years old and wanted to get out, and she was screaming and crying. At that point I was heavily pregnant and couldn't carry her. We were in a busy place and if she had run off, I would have had no chance of catching her. I got down to her level and started to hum to catch her attention and then took some really deep breaths. It took a couple of minutes, but she stopped the crying and was calm. Her brain and body are born to copy, and she did. This is something worth learning in parenting classes!

As your kids get older, they won't want to be that close to you, or they will be too big! So do this: Stand facing them, take big, exaggerated breaths, in through the nose and out through the mouth. So big that they can see your chest rise and fall. No need to ask them to copy, in fact don't even mention it. Just as the little ones innately copy so do the older ones, including teens and even adults having a panic attack. Breathing like this will calm their fight or flight reaction down quickly and innately.

The three states of emotional regulation for kids

There are three stages to emotional regulations for kids.

1. **Learn to identify their emotions.**
   Encourage kids to name their emotions or, if they can't, you can do it for them. For example, 'You look sad' or 'Wow! You look excited'. You can also talk about how you are feeling – it is a great way of extending their emotional literacy with more descriptive emotional words.

Real-life example

Mo was about six years old when his parents contacted me. He was struggling at school with academics, as well as with making friends. Teachers were having to keep a close eye on him during play times as that was usually when he exploded. When I first met Mo, he was nothing like his teachers described. First of all, they didn't tell me just how funny he was, or how bright. He did struggle with some of his school work, but he was the best card shark I ever met! I set to work on expanding his emotional vocabulary and identifying his feelings. Mo picked this up really quickly, and once he had the words to express himself, the playground fights and kicking of other kids to get their attention stopped. He had the words and the confidence to convey how he felt in a more positive way.

2. **Recognise what triggers big emotions.** Help kids identify what gets them upset. For example, 'It seems that when you don't get passed the ball in the game, you get really angry'. Not only are you helping them recognise the triggers but it also validates their feelings.

3. **Teach kids to regulate their own emotions.** I have taught three-year-olds the hand model of the brain, using words such as guard dog for the amygdala, memory box for hippocampus, and wise old owl for the prefrontal cortex. This gives them a rare insight and control over their own emotions.

Top tips for teaching kids emotional management

The more the kids are aware of their emotions and can regulate them in a healthy way, the more they can handle life's stressors. It is a skill that if mastered has a huge positive impact on not only their mental health but physical health too. More than that, they find relationships in schools, families and even future workplace easier to navigate. It helps lessen anxiety and they become more equipped to deal with life's challenges. The biggest issue for us as parents is to keep our emotions under control and have patience while we walk our kids through theirs. Here are some tools to support you in that:

1. **Get them involved in regular exercise.** Stress hormones, such as cortisol, can sit and rest in the stomach, causing some kids to complain about having a tummy ache. Any exercise can help, such as walking, team sports, or even as simple as stretching, especially yoga poses, such as boat and cat-cow. These can really help disperse cortisol and help regulate those emotions. Activity is particularly important if your child struggles with anxiety.

2. **Breathing exercises.** Big deep breaths in through the nose and out through the mouth as described earlier is great but there are many others. Here are my favourites:

   Hot chocolate breaths. Imagine you have a cup of very hot chocolate in front of you. Take a real big deep slow breath in through your nose and imagine you can smell the delicious chocolate. Then slowly release your breath through your mouth, being careful not to blow any of the imagined cream off the top hot chocolate. Do this several times, imagining you are cooling the hot chocolate as you go.

Finger breathing. Hold one hand out in front of you and make a pointing finger with the other hand. With that finger, trace around your hand. Each time the finger goes upwards, breathe in through your nose and every time it's a downward action then breathe out of your mouth. Do this until you have traced round the whole hand.

3. **Create a list.** Make a list with your child or teen of things they can do when they have flipped their lid.
4. **Go for a walk** or run.
5. **Listen to music** – get them to create their own playlist
6. **Bounce on your bed or trampoline** – even roughhousing on the floor with siblings or adults is a good way to expend that energy.
7. **Meditate.** This can be as easy as counting breaths to listening to guided meditation, so long as you are focusing on one thing at a time.
8. **Draw, sketch, doodle** or simply colour in (focusing on one thing at a time is a form of meditation).
9. **Speak to a friend** on Facetime. Chatting to someone who cares about us helps calm our nervous system and shifts our mood.
10. **Talk to an adult.** This could be an aunt, uncle, grandparent or other significant adult in their life.

A reminder! Parents and kids' champions, don't forget that it takes time to regulate. Be aware that once a child flips their lid, it takes a good thirty to forty-five minutes to reset their nervous system. During this time, we need to connect with them, hear them and give them space. Whatever has upset them, whether they are in trouble or have fallen out with someone else, we need to be respectful and give them space and time before we talk about what they have done.

thy   Confidence   Pur

Self-care   Gratitude

idence   Belonging   Empath

de   Empathy   Responsib

ction   Purpose   Self-ca

hy   Gratitude   Belonging

Responsibility   Empath

pose   Connection   Sel

Empathy   Purpose

Chapter five:
Your resilient kid

RESILIENCE CAN BE BUILT. BUT how? I hear you cry. It is made up of components that, if strengthened, can lead to protecting our kids from the bigger challenges in life. Think about each trait as a brick in a wall – the more bricks, the sturdier the wall. Not only will strengthening and adding bricks help to build resilience but it will also hardwire their brain to respond well under the pressure and everyday stress they will encounter in life. If you go to the Resources at the front of the book you can take my quiz to see how resilient your child is. The quiz will identify any gaps in their resilience which you can boost by using the tips in this section.

Courage: How do we encourage our kids to be braver?

We often talk about confidence when speaking to our kids – for example, the confidence to try something new. However, confidence is a word that doesn't quite hit the same definitions and meanings for kids as it does for adults. I prefer to talk to kids about courage. When you talk about courage, kids understand the concept of what it is to be brave – taking that risk even when it's challenging or nerve racking.

Often, through our own fear, we limit kids' opportunities to take risks. Judith Locke, PhD, in her book *The Bonsai Child*, talks about how, as parents, we are increasingly making children's lives too easy by constantly doing too much for them, producing 'Bonsai children', seemingly perfect kids raised in a very protected environment needing constant care and attention, who then go on to struggle in the real world.[18]

In the days before technology was handheld and every kid had a smartphone or tablet, they were outside playing with cousins and friends. They got into scrapes and had to sort it out themselves. They learnt boundaries and empathy along the way. We are a much more closed community now, with kids hanging out online with friends rather than meeting up in person. The chances of them having to be courageous are fewer. Kids are not climbing trees like they once were. There is a lower risk of getting hurt playing a computer game, apart from losing the replenishable number of lives.

Karen Young, psychologist and author writes, 'Kids and teens step up to expectations or down to them. Speak to the courage that is coming to life inside them, as though they are already there.'[19]

Sometimes we only need to be courageous for a few minutes, or even seconds, while we make that leap, reach out to a new friend, order our own meal, put our hand up or whatever the situation. When we were young, we thought we were fearless, but why was that? Because we knew we had people in our corner, older siblings or cousins, extended family members or even a neighbour down the street. We had people believing in us and what they say becomes our inner dialogue. I encourage parents and kids' champions to talk to our kids like the brave is already there inside them. 'I think you are great taking this step', or 'It's a brave decision you are taking, I am proud of you. I know that wasn't easy or you might not feel brave right now, but I know what doing this means to you.'

We need our kids to be brave. We throw everything at them at a critical time in their lives, when their brains and bodies are developing. We get them to move from nursery to primary, then secondary and beyond. We give them assessments, then exams, we ask them to make new friends, meet new teachers, take responsibility for a variety of things like money, equipment, and of course, themselves. All the while asking them to make decisions that will affect their entire future careers!

We need to create opportunities for them to try out being brave. One thing we adults need to remember is that it's not supposed to be comfortable. Stepping into confidence and being courageous is uncomfortable to the point that sometimes it hurts. Not majorly, but that's the point. We need to get used to being uncomfortable.

Parent cues

Walking with your kid or teen to help them experience bravery, taking steps out of their own comfort zones, doesn't have to be huge or eventful. Here are some ideas that you can easily incorporate into your days with your kids.

1. **Try new food.** Invite your kids to try a new food, whether it is a new cuisine or just a new texture. Sometimes this pays off and they add another food to their favourite list. Sometimes, not so much, but again it's a small risk and if there is no big deal made of liking or not liking it, then they will tend to do it again and again without a fuss.

2. **Get them to take the lead.** Invite your kids to order in a café or restaurant. They are in a safe environment; they are with you. It can be risky talking to strangers but only a small risk and it helps develop their self-esteem. Ordering for themselves not only builds independence but also helps when they have to read out loud in class as they get older.

3. **Tasks or chores.** Invite your kids to help around the house. I cannot stress this enough. They are never too young! It could be popping laundry in a basket when they are toddlers or emptying the dishwasher when they are a teen. If you want to access an age appropriate chore list make sure you download the many free resources that come with this book by scanning the QR code at the front of the book.

Parents often ask me why get the kids involved? It builds life skills and adds more courage bricks in their walls of resilience as they try new things, but equally as important, doing jobs around the house creates a sense of belonging and being valued in the family unit. Plus, as a bonus it helps you out. I hear all the time, 'Well it's quicker to do it myself.' Yes, it is not always going to be perfect but if you don't give them this learning opportunity now you will still be picking up after them when they are thirty-five! And let me tell you, future partners will not thank you! The extra bonus is that they start to have a belief in themselves. There is no accident that soldiers must make their bed first thing every day and that is because there is a sense of achievement at the very start of the day. If we don't create this sense of belonging and need for them in the family, they seek that elsewhere. That is why gangs are so popular with young people: they belong, they are needed. Whether we agree with gangs or not, they fulfil a gap that might be missing in that young person's life.

4. **New activities**. Try out a new activity. If you have a shy kid then go as a family so they have their safety net with them – for example you could take them to a tree-top ropes course or to a trampoline park. Even board games are good for this as playing a game like this teaches them to fail and losing is part of that feedback loop we all need to

improve. I find that boys particularly find it hard to lose face. Playing board games is a safe way to lose and get used to not winning all the time. And don't let them win every time! No one at school is going to let them win so don't be tempted to at home either.

5. **Debates.** Have debates about everything from standing up for people who are different to them to what's the best biscuit in the world. It gives your kids the courage to stand up for what they believe in and how to articulate their voice when needed.

One of our family values is being an ally to others. I was born in South Africa to white parents and I have been well aware of the privilege that was (and is) afforded to me. It is important to have those kinds of conversations around the dinner table. What can we do for others? Who doesn't have the same opportunities or privileges in life as us? How can we stand up for others? Take the time to talk about issues such as Black Lives Matter (download the extra resources that accompany this book for help with this). All of this takes courage – not just from the kids but from us too. Don't shy away from other debates either, such as sexism or disablism (again, see extra resources). Debates like this are important as it increases their empathy and self-awareness for everyone in the community, but also don't underestimate listening to your kids – being open to our children's views is meaningful for not only

our growth but so our kids know we are
listening.

6. **Admitting we are wrong**. An integral part
of courage is admitting when we are wrong.
We don't often shine a light on this, and
young people see the opposite modelled as
governments all over the world shy away
from admitting their wrong doings every
day in the news. As a society we are waiting
to catch people out instead of respecting
them for owning up. Research shows that
although it is a dent in our egos to admit
being at fault, it is extremely important in
strengthening our relationships and growing
our empathy, sympathy and of course,
listening skills.[20]

Real-life example

There was a bust up between two boys – let's call them
Jack and Dan. It was in the first term of the first year of
high school. Jack already had a reputation – it was the
third time he'd hit another student in as many weeks.
Dan said he was sticking up for a friend when he got hit.

On the face of it, and from their statements to
school, Jack is in the wrong. After all, Jack's already
got a reputation as a troublemaker and Dan was
clearly in the wrong place at the wrong time. Dan
was seen as a good kid – polite, engaging in class
and with plenty of friends. Dan was asked several
times if there was any more to the story and each
time a little bit more came out. Eventually, when

CCTV was viewed, it showed Dan pushing Jack into a wall, and then Jack coming out swinging. Dan was given every opportunity to admit being wrong but didn't. Why?

There are several reasons:

1. **It is hard to admit you are wrong.** Shame and embarrassment are powerful triggers in our fight or flight reaction, which were present for both boys.
2. **There was a ready-made scapegoat.** Who is going to believe Jack, already labelled by peers and teachers as a troublemaker? The chances of getting away with it were high for Dan. (A pity he didn't know about the CCTV.)
3. **The worry of losing respect** from teachers and peers.

So how do we handle it as parents or educators when the truth finally comes out?

Firstly, acknowledge the good part, for there usually is one. Dan was sticking up for a friend. Secondly, recognise that Dan didn't admit he was wrong, and how important that is. People receive more respect when wrongdoing is admitted than when they lie. Thirdly, ask Dan to acknowledge and walk through what would have happened to Jack on his third strike and how admitting that he started the confrontation is actually being an ally to Jack too.

I would also suggest that you ask the kids to pick the consequences of their own actions. In this case, Dan chose no phone for a week. When asked how that makes it up with Jack, he realised the two weren't connected, that he was making it about what he had done wrong and not thinking about Jack, so he offered to write an apology letter to Jack in addition to his phone ban.

This teaches Dan two things – responsibility and accountability for his actions. Just because you don't think you'll get caught doesn't mean that it's ok. It is also a lesson to Jack, that just because you get into a pattern of behaviour – for whatever reason – doesn't mean all people are willing to let you take the fall. This episode helped to build character and strengthen the relationship and resilience in both boys. As a side note, it was important for the adults around Jack to see incidents in isolation rather than 'here he goes again!' After doing some work with them, they have looked at why Jack comes out fighting and things have settled down. Jack knows he has someone in his corner he can go to, and he doesn't have to tackle everything alone.

Things we can do to improve courage and confidence

1. **Give permission for imperfection.**
2. **Talk as if they're already brave** and courageous – praise effort rather than achievement/results.
3. **Allow them to problem solve** rather than you stepping in.
4. **Let them know it will be uncomfortable** – but that is where courage grows.

Empathy: Can we teach it?

'Could a greater miracle take place than for us to look through each other's eyes for an instant.' – Henry David Thoreau[21]

As we have just seen in the real-life example, Dan had a moral dilemma to face. Does he admit what he did or let Jack take the blame? These everyday dilemmas not only build a kid's character but are often based on how much empathy we feel for the other person. Once Dan realised there was much more to Jack's story than he understood, and he knew the serious-ness for Jack, he became very empathetic and made friends, taking full responsibility. Jack and Dan are still friends today.

What's the difference between sympathy and empathy?

In her TED talk Dr Brené Brown explains the dif-ference between the two. She states that sympathy is to see someone in a deep hole but remaining on higher ground and talking to them from above. In contrast, empathy is feeling what they might be feel-ing, climbing down into the hole to sit beside them, making themselves vulnerable too and establishing a connection with them. The empathetic person will recognise the person's struggle without minimising it or dismissing it.[22]

In essence, empathy is about walking in someone else's shoes, an appreciation of another person's point of view or situation, even if it's only for a moment in time. Research shows a clear correlation between resilience and empathy. Those kids who have better empathy skills are the ones who have improved social relationships, are better at resolving conflict and are quicker to bounce back after trauma.

Why is it important to give children opportunities to practise their empathy? Because this is where character is built.

A few years ago, we were planning a trip to India, and we invited our in-laws with us. At the time the kids were probably about five and seven. I mentioned to my mother-in-law that I had booked to go to a local orphanage. She was horrified. 'The kids are on holiday,' she cried, as if it was a chore. In reality, she probably didn't want to face poverty and the hard emotions that go with that when we think of children in an orphanage. I said we had it planned as a family and the kids had already picked clothes that were too small and teddies to take with them.

When the day arrived, my mother-in-law decided she wanted to come along, much to my surprise. We arrived and my kids played with the kids there while we spoke to the adults and teachers about the kind of work they did and funds they were raising. It was a beautiful sight to see kids playing together with no language, just fun and laughter. As our visit was coming to an end, my mother-in-law took out her cheque book (remember them?), quietly wrote out a cheque and gave it to the head of the orphanage. We chatted to our kids about how lucky we were to have a family and nice things and they spoke about the fun they had and how lovely their new friends were. There was a humble atmosphere as we all weighed up our privilege that day. Later on, my mother-in-law thanked us for taking her but asked what made us think of going? I said to her, it's not always about travelling hundreds of miles to go to an orphanage but **how do we expect our kids to help others if they only see themselves?** It is our responsibility as parents not to pretend everything is perfect in the world. After all, it's the kids that will change it!

Back to the brain

Neuroimaging studies show that the same areas of the brain are activated when we experience our own emotions as when we observe the emotion of someone else. It doesn't matter if it is sadness, pain or happiness that our brain is observing, our brain reacts as though it is happening to us. More than that, it brings in other areas of the brain which control social interaction, emotional self-control and moral reasoning. This again leads to empathy and development of character – who doesn't want their child to have that moral compass?[23,24]

This is where we come in.

Shame versus guilt

In days gone by, shame lead the parenting way, but it can have a lasting effect and cause great damage for generations. There is a high correlation between those children who are raised with a high level of shame being more likely to struggle with depression, not finish school and get involved in more risky behaviours such as drugs, alcohol and underage sex.

Let's look at the difference between shame and guilt.

Guilt is defined by the *Cambridge Dictionary* as a 'feeling of worry or unhappiness that you have because you have done something wrong'.[25]

Shame is defined by the *Oxford Dictionary* as a 'feeling of humiliation or distress caused by the consciousness of wrong or foolish behaviour'.[26]

This is Brené Brown's, as previously mentioned, field of expertise – she is a shame researcher. She states, 'Shame says **I am bad**, whereas Guilt says **I made a bad choice**'. Can you see the subtle difference? Shaming our kids integrates the negative behaviour into their identity, part of who they are, while guilt focuses on their behaviour – that is, what they've done. If we don't want our kids to follow a riskier path through life, we need to focus on their behaviour rather than shame them personally.

Parent cues

How do we encourage empathy in our kids? Can it be learnt? For little ones we can only encourage empathy when they understand they are separate from us. Before the age of two, kids think that their main caregiver and themselves are one person and will actively point to the caregiver in a mirror when talking about themselves.[27] Here are some ways that we can teach and encourage empathy, even from the earliest years.

1. **Talk emphatically.** For example, 'You look scared, are you OK?' 'This makes me sad to see you upset,' giving them examples of you being aware of their feelings.

2. **Discuss other people's feelings.** 'Harry dropped his ice cream – he looks sad.' This is a great way to start labelling emotions in conversation but also encouraging them to see it from Harry's point of view.
3. **Encourage kids to help others,** whether it's picking up each other's toys or clothes or picking up litter locally.

When it comes to older kids, you can add some more complicated thinking and experiences.

1. Invite your older kids to **think about 'the shoe on the other foot'.**

Real-life example

Dylan has overheard a conversation about nicknames in his older sister's year group. He then sees one of the people discussed and mentions it to them, much to his older sister's embarrassment. Now luckily it wasn't anything bad but it has caused issues between the siblings. Dylan can't see what he has done wrong. It was pointed out that if his sister had gone up to one of his friends and said he was talking about them, how would he feel? He now understands the embarrassment and apologises to his older sister.

2. **Get them involved in community or charity projects.** This allows them to reflect on their position in life in comparison, especially when it comes to talks about race and inequality. It's often a hard topic but

don't shy away. Research shows that when
we talk about inclusivity it naturally boosts
our empathy.[28]

3. **Talk about what we have in common
with people different to us.** The more we
feel we have in common, the more empathy
we have with them.

Gratitude: The antidote to entitlement

Gratitude also has a role in building resilience. I've
heard many conversations about entitlement and lack
of gratitude, especially when it comes to young people.
Let's talk about these two separately for a moment
and then see how they intertwine.

Entitlement is seen when a person can't distin-
guish between what they need and what they want.
Psychologists even have a label for it – the entitlement complex. When we are toddlers, we have this
in abundance – it's the tantrum throwing kind of
behaviour that is seen as part of development. Parents
get that sympathetic look in the supermarket, as the
tantruming toddler is scooped up, eyes and snotty
nose wiped, and the toddler is appeased in some way,
whether it's a toy or a treat, or they are told not today
but rewarded with cuddles and attention. At this age,
the toddler thinks they are the centre of the world
and often, at this time, they are.

As we grow, we learn patience and how to ask
for things without throwing ourselves on the floor.
However, sometimes we learn to throw a tantrum
in a more cultured way. We make demands or have
expectations about the people and world around us.

In young people, it could be getting a mobile phone, expecting lifts, or presuming that clothes are magically cleaned and returned to their wardrobe.

How does this happen? All too easily. I am not saying that all young people have an entitlement complex, by any stretch. Most young people I encounter are gracious, humble and want to learn. What I am doing by mentioning it here, is calling us out, as adults, on how we contribute to it. You see when we constantly give in or don't establish healthy boundaries, then a natural consequence is for our kids to think they are entitled.

Kids need to know you are the leader of the pack. If this is not clear, then of course they will act as if they are the centre of the universe – who wouldn't? This hierarchy is important for several reasons.

1. It stops the sense of entitlement.
2. It teaches them respect for adults and authority.
3. It helps them feel safe and secure.

When you lead, they follow and will turn to you for guidance when they are overwhelmed or unsure of a situation. If they don't have that faith in you because you change your mind, or defer to them, or you aren't stable, they start to doubt you! As adults in their life, we need to be their touchstone, the safe haven they return to in times of worries or stress. What we don't want to see is them turning to peers to get that guidance or worse still, taking on those adult responsibilities and risks when their brain is not fully developed.

Kids who are overindulged and over-parented, are going to struggle later in life when clean clothes don't magically appear and they don't get paid if they don't turn up to work. It is natural to not want to see your kids struggle but there is a sense that we have taken it too far, that in trying to avoid them feeling discomfort or failure we take away their opportunity to make their own mistakes and learn from them. In essence, we take away their ability to build their resilience. We can't shelter them from life – sadly, bad things happen in everyone's lives, and we need to equip our kids to deal with bad situations, not hide from them. We know, though, that we establish boundaries and teach our children these skills from a good place. Amy McCready writes in her book, *The Me, Me, Me Epidemic*, 'too much of a good thing can result in kids who always expect to get what they want when they want it'.[29]

How do we ensure that our kids don't become entitled?

We start by stopping doing things for our kids which they can do themselves and if they can't do it, teach them! When kids learn to do things for themselves, it not only gives them confidence, as we have seen earlier, and gives them the courage to try new things, but it also empowers them for the future. Start simple – what skills in the home can your kids do now? If you were laid up with a broken leg, would they be able to hang the washing out, wash the pots, cook a meal, phone the doctors, do the simple things that keep the household running?

Secondly, we teach them to be grateful – perhaps not to the extremes of taking them to an orphanage, but general everyday gratitude.

The benefits of gratitude

Research has shown that gratitude has a major role in building resilience. Other benefits include greater and more consistent levels of happiness, more enjoyment of experiences, improvement in health and building stronger relationships.

Gratitude is a recognition and appreciation of what we have. It helps us become more optimistic. For young people who look at all the worries of the world on social media, whether it is local crime, wars breaking out around the world or the cost-of-living crisis, they need this. Hell, we all need this.

Studies have also shown that kids who express their gratitude sleep better, are less aggressive, have increased self-esteem and are better able to cope with stress.

How do we help kids to be more grateful?

We talked about the importance of jobs around the house earlier in this book, so thank your kids every time they help! Model gratitude for them. It doesn't matter if they have set the table or cooked dinner, saying thank you leaves them feeling valued and appreciated. Also let them hear you thank others for the coffee they serve you or for driving the bus you just rode.

Just be aware that kids under six have to be constantly reminded. Manners don't become automatic until they are around eight-years-old, when they begin to hone their empathy skills.

Parent cues

Walking with your kid or teen to encourage gratitude doesn't have to be a big change in how you live your life. Here are some ideas that you can easily incorporate into your days with your kids.

1. Round the table, in the car or on a walk, **talk about three things you are grateful for today.**
2. **Start a gratitude jar.** Write things periodically down that you are grateful for and pop them in a jar and open on Christmas or New Year.
3. **Perform Random Acts of Kindness** (RAK). The benefits of carrying out a RAK is huge! Doing something kind for someone else increases happy hormones like oxytocin and serotonin, which help us stay calm, sleep better, and feel happier as well as boosting endorphins, the brain's natural pain killer. If we do one act of kindness not only does it have these great effects for us, but also for the person on the receiving end. The bonus is that anyone witnessing the RAK also receives these unexpected benefits and they are only the observer.
4. **Donating outgrown items.** Invite the kids to sort out toys or clothes to give to a charity shop. This works well if they take the items to the shop, as the volunteers are usually very grateful and that helps the kids feel good about themselves.

5. **Raise money for charity.** An easy way to do this is to participate in a sponsored activity. Choose a charity that might be close to your family – get the kids involved in choosing.

6. **Buy a coffee for the person behind you in the queue** while the kids are there so they can see you role modelling random acts of kindness.

7. **Label the emotions.** Talk about how it makes you feel to help others and ask the kids what it felt like watching another person benefit from kindness. The action doesn't have to be big – holding the door or lift for someone has the same effects as helping a neighbour with their bags.

8. **Start a gratitude journal.** This doesn't have to be a weighty tome. Younger children can draw something and older children can write a sentence or two about what they are grateful for that day. With teens, encourage them to take photos with their phones and save them into a gratitude folder.

The scientific benefits are undeniable and why would we not want to empower our kids to be happier, healthier, have more self-worth and live longer? It also helps them refocus on what they have rather than what they have not.

Purpose: Finding what matters to them

It's a question kids and teens are always asking themselves. 'Who am I?' They seek out experiences to define their likes and dislikes, strengths and weaknesses, who their friends are and who they don't want to hang out with. Understanding more about purpose and contribution helps them answer this question.

The best way to help our kids and teens discover their purpose is to ask ourselves, 'what matters to our kids?' As adults we often ask ourselves, 'what is our purpose?' Then we get lost in the busyness of life – our jobs, the home, the kids. How do kids find out what matters to them, what their purpose is?

Well, firstly, those kids who develop a sense of purpose, unsurprisingly, have good emotional literacy and social skills.

Secondly, they need to feel that they matter, that they are heard and valued.

The impact that these have, along with a sense of purpose, has an impact on their motivation and contribution to their community and is so worthwhile.

Real-life example

Freya was struggling at 6th form college. Her exams hadn't gone that well and her results were much lower than predicted. Her parents were worried, not that she was particularly depressed but that she lacked motivation for anything. Whilst talking to them, Freya would often say, 'What's the point?' She spent lots of hours in her room on her phone or watching box sets, and if she did eat with the rest of the family, she refused to help clear away. When she did do any homework, it was the bare minimum – often tutors were chasing her for it, or she was asking for an extension. She was the youngest in the family, with older siblings already working. Freya had no sense of purpose or her role within the family. Whenever she was asked to contribute, she refused and so her parents didn't enforce anything. When her siblings wanted to spend time with her, she either refused or went and was in a terrible mood. There were no expectations in the family unit on contributing or on behaviour. We all have a pattern of behaviour, and we stick with that pattern if it works for us. Freya's seemingly negative patterns of behaviour were getting her attention so there was no motivation to change – she was being noticed! The fact she was miserable most of the time, dealing with the stress of tutors chasing or parents nagging her, was not enough of a motivator to change the way she interacted with her world.

As adults we find it very difficult to understand why kids choose a negative path. 'Why don't they just act as they are asked/told?' The better question to ask is, 'Why would they change, if it works for them, if they are getting what they want?' After conversations with Freya and her parents, we talked about getting positive attention (kids don't see the difference between positive and negative attention – it's all attention!), carving a role within the family, helping and consequences of not helping. Freya expected lifts and money for make-up. Mum and dad wanted to give Freya what she wanted but saw that the expectation from her was at a cost. She was not motivated to do anything because she got what she needed without doing anything to earn it. When her parents realised this, they began having a meeting on a Sunday setting out expectations, letting Freya and the rest of the family know what was expected that week: checking who needed lifts, who was responsible for cooking dinner and other tasks. It worked really well. Freya became more involved in the family and became more motivated to do her college work as well. We have great intentions when we actively try not to expect too much of our kids, but it can often backfire, leading to no expectations – and the kids to wonder where they fit in the family!

Parent cues

It can seem a little vague to try, as parents and champions, to encourage a sense of purpose in our kids. But we can encourage a sense of purpose for now, help them to find their place in the world for right now, not for all time. Here are some ways to do that.

1. **Managing emotions.** It all comes back to this! Teaching them how to manage their emotions and build social skills, including empathy, are definite building blocks to finding purpose and a place in the world.
2. **Learning about inspirational people.** Being influenced by other people who have a purpose, whether it's a local person who has held a charity event in the community or a high-profile celebrity who has overcome adversity is a great way to practically see what can be possible. Talking to your kid about how these inspirational people have got to where they have, what they are bringing to the community and discuss how that then gives others permission to have a

go too. It's that old adage, 'If we can't see it, we can't be it.'

3. **Variety.** When I was young, my mum complained that whatever activity I tried, I would give up just after she bought the uniform! I tried Brownies, netball, horse riding – mum was right, it's a long list! As a parent or kids' champion, don't lose hope and don't spend a tonne of money, ask for a free trial if it's an extra-curricular activity. Often at secondary school, there are lots of free after-school or lunchtime sessions, ranging from chess to sports to drama. You can expose your kids to a variety of experiences through reading and writing, drawing, games and problem solving. One simple game of Cluedo with my eldest set off her love of murder mystery and, as I write this book, her future goal is to study law or forensics.

4. **Listen.** What are your kids asking questions about? What topics are coming up in conversation? What are they choosing to watch or listen to? Tune in to their thoughts and interests for hints to help them find their purpose and place in life.

5. **Goals.** Setting small targets is great. They help build confidence, internal motivation and promote an optimistic mindset. Small goals can also control the feeling of overwhelm around life's big decisions. I find students in year ten and eleven start to get anxious about exams, A levels, what

to do for their career, will they be able to get a house – their minds go into overdrive. Setting goals can remind them to take it one step at a time, rather than worry about big life decisions.

Contribution: how can they give back?

Lots of our purpose or meaning in life can be found in how we contribute to our family or the wider community. This is why allocating jobs around the house is more than saving you from emptying the dishwasher – it is building a sense of worth for your kids' character and contributing to the family unit. Young people who get involved in the wider community not only develop a sense of purpose but build skills that will help them thrive in other communities such as university or the workplace.

How can helping your kids to see where they can contribute and allowing them to contribute build their resilience?

1. **It's not about you!** Supporting kids to contribute means they see beyond themselves. Beyond their smartphones or gaming consoles, beyond going out with friends or what to wear. They learn that the world doesn't revolve around them – it is the perfect antidote to entitlement as they learn their place in a wider world.
2. **Feedback.** Kids who contribute get that immediate feedback of gratitude that isn't just from a family member. ('You have to

say that because you love me.') They feel that they matter and what they are doing is making a difference. When young people are surrounded by gratitude, they have the chance to thrive in their own right. These positive messages not only build their resilience but help to insulate them from negative comments in the future. It is harder to dent someone's self-esteem if it is built on strong foundations and, when kids contribute, it's not just the foundations you have laid, but foundations the community as a whole has contributed to laying.

3. **Skills.** Not only may your kids discover a new purpose or interest but they could find a new talent or learn a new skill through volunteering. Kids will also learn how to interact with strangers, practice using manners and speaking politely and constantly improving their communication skills. Invariably our family is involved in many community projects from fundraising at school, volunteer awards and local TEDx events. My kids have learned skills such as upselling, leaflet distribution, looking after smaller kids, hair braiding, counting stock and money, greeting the public and writing social media posts to name but a few.

Real-life example

Grace needed to volunteer to complete her Duke of Edinburgh Award. She volunteered at a local children's cancer charity. She was told that the duties would be helping with events, joining in with the kids and cleaning up afterwards. On her first day, she connected with a couple of younger girls. She helped with their activities, chatted and listened to them. The look of admiration on their faces was just magic. Not only did Grace go back twice more that week (despite it being the week before her mock exams – practice papers) she said it felt great, not just because she felt like she had really made a difference for the young girls, but also the adult staff had praised her for using her initiative. It gave her a real confidence boost.

4. **Confidence.** We have already touched on confidence but I think it is worth repeating here. The confidence kids gain from learning new skills outside the home propels them to take on new and bigger challenges with more confidence. Research suggests:[30]

   a. Kids and teens who volunteer for one hour a week are fifty percent less likely to engage in risky behaviour such as drugs, alcohol, underage sex and so on.
   b. They are more likely to have higher self-esteem and higher academic achievement than those who don't.
   c. Those young volunteers are more likely to have a positive work ethic and have a feeling of social responsibility, even going so far as being more likely to vote than those who don't volunteer.

      d. They usually earn more money when
         employed than those who haven't
         volunteered.

      e. Kids and teens who volunteer will be
         more accepting of other ages, cultures
         and languages too.

5. **Help.** A real strong benefit for me is that
kids who volunteer are more likely to ask
for help when they need it. As a teen it
is particularly hard to ask for help – they
feel like they should already know it, be it.
As a society we don't generally encourage
reaching out and asking for help. When
kids see the difference they make in the
world and their community, they see their
value and how good it actually feels to help
others. (See also random acts of kindness on
page 81 for just how good it feels.) In turn,
volunteering takes away the shame in asking
for help when they are in need. They don't
view themselves as a burden but that the
person they are turning to for help is there
because they choose to be.

Parent cues

This is another way we can walk our kids through
this and encourage contribution. It can take some
research, but that's part of the fun! And what better
way to role model it for them but volunteer side by
side.

1. **Start small.** Get your kids involved in recycling in the home or litter picking at the park. Explain how it makes a difference in the community, country and the world as a whole. This can be done from a young age.

2. **Look in the local community.** What's going on? What is needed? Is there a local food bank where they could volunteer? Helping others who are less privileged than they are may well give them perspective on how lucky they are and add a hefty serving of gratitude there.

   Scouts and guides are great at getting kids involved in local community projects (see additional resources with this book). However, you don't need to sign up to get involved in your local community. Look at local care homes, community events, neighbours, or schools and nurseries. They may need anything from shopping, litter picking to painting murals.

3. Invite your kids to **sort books and donate what they've grown out of** reading to a local school or library. You could also enquire about volunteering to read to younger children.

Mahatma Gandhi said, **'The best way to find yourself is to lose yourself in the service of others.'** Giving kids the opportunity to be a part of something bigger than themselves is giving them the opportunity for them to see their best selves.

Responsibility: Allowing our kids to be accountable

There are several parts to responsibility, but first let's define what we mean by the word responsible – it is simply being accountable for our actions.

When we talk about responsibility and kids, the key thing is that it is them (not us) who are responsible for their behaviour, their belongings and their actions. However, don't we also want them to be responsible for their feelings? To own them and to learn to regulate them? As parents we often try to distract them away from their feelings, because we want to stop them hurting or solve their problem, but we are not allowing them to feel all the emotions. Sometimes sitting with discomfort is the best thing they can do to learn what to do next or how it can be different in the future.

How do we as adults encourage irresponsibility?

All too easily! Things that we do and say naturally (or to try to make our kids feel better) are often not encouraging responsibility in our kids.

- We excuse bad behaviour by saying things such as 'They're tired' or 'They need to eat.'
- We do school projects or homework for them. I once saw a parent make a wooden boat and pass it off as their five-year-old's work.
- We blame others such as friends, teachers or the system for the way they have behaved.
- We do things for them, including life skills such as washing, ironing and cooking instead of teaching them to do it themselves.

- We give them money without teaching them the accountability that goes with managing it. This includes giving them expensive belongings, especially now when many kids have got smartphones, worth hundreds of pounds, in their back pocket.

I am not suggesting that we go back to the way it used to be, when the eldest child almost assumed full responsibility and looked after the younger children in the family. However, the responsibility and expectation that used to be laid on the eldest often propelled them into achievement and leadership roles. Did you know that twenty-three out of twenty-five astronauts in NASA are the eldest sibling – the other two are only children.

Educator and author, Michelle Mitchell, wrote, 'Responsibility can't be learnt if someone else takes the pressure for us.'[31] When we don't give our kids the opportunity to be responsible, they miss out.

Real-life example

Hannah is five years old. She has a new younger brother in the house. Mum feels guilty that she doesn't give Hannah as much attention since the baby came along. When dressing Hannah every morning for school, she will often say, 'You need to learn how to dress yourself one day' though continues to do it, sometimes for speed as well as guilt. After PE at school, Hannah struggles to get dressed herself. Her peers are quicker and get outside to play faster – she must wait for the teaching assistant to finish helping another child who has additional needs. Hannah gets embarrassed and will often cry or get angry that she can't dress herself. Of course, it is much easier for mum to dress Hannah, but there is a need here that is not being addressed. Hannah's fight and flight response is being activated when she gets embarrassed that she can't dress herself. She is also missing quality time with her peers who are off playing while Hannah waits for assistance.

Real-life example

Laura did really well on her A Levels and got a place on her desired course at university. During the first term, she really struggled with anxiety around the course work and living away from home. Mum was concerned she would give up in the first term. Part of my job is to help Laura unpick why – it turns out it was because her mum often sat and did her revision and homework with her. Mum, coming from a good place, wanted to support her daughter and give her the motivation to complete projects. However, for Laura, the motivation to work was to please mum (external motivation) rather than to complete homework for the reward of finishing it and her own pride (internal motivation). Furthermore, Laura actually struggled with how to do the work alone without her mum there to explain, so in lectures she hadn't listened properly, not taking on the responsibility and as a result she was getting behind with work. When I looked at this with Laura, we came up with a plan of how to catch up and I explained the importance to mum of guiding her rather than doing work for her. Laura did the work, began to be proud of what she was accomplishing and began to enjoy university more.

Laura rarely rings home with assignment problems now and continues to do well at university.

Unconscious messages

Looking under the surface of the words, Hannah's mum is saying that Hannah isn't capable of dressing herself, when actually, with a couple of practices and some spare time, Hannah will be more than capable to dress herself.

Laura's mum thought she was helping during A levels but hadn't quite realised she had taken the responsibility away from Laura for doing the work, planning to a deadline and all the other things that we learn when we manage our own workload. The relief when Laura became responsible for her own university work was tangible for mum.

Parent cues

What else are we saying to our kids when we don't teach them responsibility? We do have to teach this. What happens in your house? If the kids make a sandwich for themselves, who cleans up?

1. **Number one rule.** If kids mess it up, they clean it up. In our house we have a toilet downstairs. On the side of the sink is a little hook where the hand towel lives to use after washing your hands. When the youngest has been in there, the towel is often screwed up on the side, or worse – on the floor. I know you're thinking I should be grateful he has

washed his hands! And I am. As easy as it would be to put the towel back myself, I call my youngest to put it back. It isn't a big deal but if I keep doing it for him, where the towel belongs won't stick in his brain. I am also teaching him that if he doesn't do it someone else has to pick up after him and that is not how life works.

2. **Routines.** Daily tasks, such as making the bed in the morning and putting toys away build the foundations for good study habits and work ethic in the future. It also gives kids a sense of pride in something they have achieved – however small. As mentioned previously, it is the reason soldiers must make their bed first thing.

3. **Encourage repairing relationships.** When siblings argue, our first reaction is to get them to say sorry. But if they are not ready to apologise, then they likely won't mean it and it won't do anything for the aggrieved party. Try listening to how the kids feel and help them work through their emotions. If they still don't feel like apologising, then ask how else they can make it up. This is teaching them that their actions or treatment of others comes at a cost and that relationships have the potential to break and may need to be repaired. Maybe instead of apologising, helping the sibling with homework or chores restores the relationship. This is true accountability in action, they are responsible for the repair,

and they have an opportunity to problem solve this and use this with friends.

4. **Don't replace it**. If your kids damage or lose something, don't just replace it. Give them the opportunity to earn towards the replacement. Smartphones are the biggest commodity most of our kids have. Could you imagine having something in your pocket at the age of eleven worth hundreds of pounds? With that comes responsibility and great life lessons. Here are the phone rules I use with my kids and recommend to clients:

   • It's not your phone, it belongs to me. This means a few things. When I ring or text, you answer or call back as soon as possible. The main reason for a phone is to be able to get hold of them. When parents ring, it's usually for a reason.

   • I can check on your messages anytime, so don't change the passcode. This is not to be nosey and see the latest gossip, it's more for their protection. This rule is particularly for younger kids and teens. Most of our kids don't know life without access to a smartphone. I was twenty-two when I bought my first mobile. As adults who knew life before mobile phones, even we struggle to put our devices away and pay attention to what's happening around us.

Real-life example

James was in a year group chat. One of the boys was calling another boy, let's call him Michael, 'gay'. Michael defended himself but a few others jumped in. James decided to be an ally and stand up for Michael, saying it was 'nobody's business', and 'what if he was' and to 'stop being homophobic.' James then received private messages from the instigator saying he was gay as well. He was sworn at, and more. James didn't share this with his parents. Even worse, it was a close friend who had started this abuse to Michael and then James. The boy who sent these messages was in the same year group James would see these boys in school every day. Once this came to light and was reported to school a couple of things happened. James was praised for being an ally to his friend. Mum and dad could also talk through what happened with James, discussing the emotions behind it and finding out how James felt and what he wanted to do. It was reported to school not just because Michael was facing this harassment, but also so the boy sending the messages could be spoken to about why he was sending these messages and take responsibility for the impact it would have on both boys.

5. **If you lose it you need to replace it.** When your kids grow up and live on their own, no one will come round and replace things they have broken or, if they hit another car when driving, it will be their responsibility. Allow them to be able to work towards replacing an item. That way they will be more careful

of and grateful for their items – don't let life lessons become a shock.

6. **Family meetings.** These are a great way of modelling responsibility. If the idea of a family meeting is new to you, check out the book resources for guidance on running these. On Sunday evening over dinner, we take out the calendar and discuss what we have on as a family over the next week. It is invariably dance classes, rugby games, after-school clubs, friends coming over and work for me and the hubby. We look at who needs a lift, who is responsible for cooking dinner on what nights (the kids take a night each). This not only clearly lays out expectations and responsibility but teaches kids time management and commitment too. This routine helps them feel more secure, they are not left wondering who is doing what and they take a turn contributing towards the family unit. If they ever house share or live with a partner in the future, it will make that transition much easier.

7. **Blame-free environment.** Let's face it, we are all human, we all make mistakes, and it's natural to want to blame someone. However, blaming someone doesn't fix the mistake. It simply makes everyone more defensive and kids more likely to lie. Yes, with blame we are actually encouraging them to lie to us!

Blame as a response is natural because it makes us feel more in control and therefore safer in a situation that is totally out of our control. Researcher Brené Brown writes, 'Blame is a discharging of discomfort and pain.'[32] It is us releasing our anger. It is the direct opposite of accountability. She goes on to say that being accountable is not only a vulnerable act but a resilient one too. Think about the language you use. 'Who did this … ?' 'Whose fault is this … ?' Does it really matter? Try out 'We need to get this cleaned up in time for dinner – who is going to help?' Or 'Let's work out how to sort this mess so we can go out.' Blaming kids triggers their fight, flight or freeze response rather than encouraging them to engage with problem solving.

Real-life example

Tom often wouldn't take responsibility. It didn't matter whether he was playing on the iPad for too long, not brushing his teeth, not cleaning up after himself or not doing homework. Whenever he messed up, his parents would always ask why and then a shouting match would begin where he would deny it and lie. They would blame him and bring up other times he hadn't been responsible – it became a cycle and nothing changed. When we looked at the language that was used there was a lot of blame being bandied around, not just by his parents but Tom too. 'It's your fault that happened, you didn't remind me.' When we looked at how to speak to Tom without blame, he began to own up and take responsibility but without embarrassment and the feeling of losing face. The questions changed to 'What help do you need Tom? What do you need to do before you leave for school?' and 'What else do you need to do before you can relax for the evening?' This way, Tom's parents are helping Tom to solve the problem and wire his brain to remember in the future. Also, it helped when they voiced taking responsibility for their own language, as Tom could see and hear it.

8. **Pay them!** While it is good to expect our kids to help do specific jobs around the house and how important it is for them to have this responsibility, I give my kids extra jobs, ones that I don't expect them to do on a regular basis, such as washing the car or rearranging the kitchen cupboards. I do this for two reasons. Firstly, they know their other jobs are them contributing to the house, and secondly, they learn that they must follow through and complete the job if they want to get paid – that is real-life responsibility.

   I started work at fourteen with my nanna when she was a manager at a well-known bakery. I wasn't legally working there but I used to help out and my nanna used to pay me out of her own money. By the time I was sixteen I knew every job on the floor, from baking the pasties, making the sandwiches, merchandising the stock, cleaning the shop, working out the rota and sorting the wages. Now it wasn't easy, being the boss's granddaughter, but I learnt fast. The minute I turned sixteen I was taken on as a Saturday kid and in the summer I earned a tonne of cash because I could do any role in the shop. I bloody loved having my own money and can still remember the first pair of Reebok trainers I bought with my first pay packet. That kind of memory is something only kids can earn for themselves. Parents often complain that kids don't see the value of money – we need to give them the opportunity to learn.

Self-care and health

If we look past general things, such as how to wash yourself and brush your teeth, did your parents show you how to take care of yourself? I mean really take care of yourself? It is important that we show our kids how we take care of ourselves and equally teach them how to take care of themselves.

When you hear self-care in the media, it is often associated with long luxurious baths or massages with fancy oils. These are the messages our kids are getting bombarded with and so they don't think self-care really applies to them.

What I think they need to know is stuff we probably weren't taught. Self-care is about being at your best, whatever the task or whoever you are with, which isn't some sleep-deprived zombie, with hair sprayed to within an inch of its life with dry shampoo.

It's learning to listen to your body when it is tired, hungry or thirsty and honouring that. It's not watching another episode of the latest boxset knowing we have a big day tomorrow.

I understand that the practicalities and the definition of self-care changes with age. The expectations we have for our primary-aged kids to care for themselves look very different to what we want and expect for our teens and again very different to ourselves as full-grown adults.

Let's start with the basics.

1. **Hygiene.** Of course, washing, showering, cleaning teeth, hair the whole thing – but, as discussed previously, it takes a while for them to cotton on that these responsibilities are a daily occurrence!

But let's go deeper.

2. **Nutrition.** We want our kids to understand nutrition and the role it plays in feeding and strengthening their mind and body. Eating snacks or fast food all day isn't going to help them in the long run, although eating a balanced diet with occasional treats at the drive thru is fine.

3. **Water.** Drinking plenty of water throughout the day helps our brains and bodies to function. Side note: Research has found that students who drink water during exams score five percent higher than those who don't! Now there is an incentive.

4. **Energy.** We want our kids to understand the importance of energy and how to direct their energy. For instance, kids who are more introverted often get 'peopled out' if they

have too much interaction socially. It often drains them. Extroverted kids often get their energy topped up when they interact with others. The danger for them is that their energy is often drained away with school drama or conflict. They get worn out when they get pulled into friendship issues or 'he said, she said' scenarios. Being aware of their energy and boundaries is an act of self-care.

5. **Comparison.** Particularly in an age of Instagram, Snapchat and BeReal it is hard for kids to not compare themselves to their peers. Unfortunately, they also compare themselves to Internet stars, who get paid to create amazing content that is often filtered and striving for perfection. This comparison trap can lead to damaging their own self-esteem. Teaching your kids to not compare themselves to others is a form of self-care. Knowing their strengths and what they may need to work on gives a stronger confidence and self-identity.

6. **Online gaming and social media.** These platforms are set up to return easy rewards. Rewards come thick and fast when playing games to boost the dopamine hits in the pleasure centre of the brain. It is no wonder kids love playing them as they get constant rewards and this can lead to being addicted to the feeling. In contrast, if we look at social media platforms, when kids post on social media, for example, Instagram, the platform withholds some of the reactions and comments, in a drip-feeding style, so the

person will keep returning to the platform to check. Again, this promotes addiction. Am I saying that technology is bad? Absolutely not! It's a gift of the golden age for kids and adults alike. However, we do need to heed the addictive nature of it. Teaching our kids to regulate their tech intake will without a doubt boost their self-care and actively promote emotional regulation.

7. **Sleep.** We are more likely to get stressed about the small stuff if we haven't had a good night's sleep. It can have a profound effect on our mental health if we don't get enough. Sleep is not just about resting – it is also the time that our brains process our memories from the day, consolidate our learning and heal our physical bodies. Here's a quick guide to the amount of sleep needed by age:
    - Toddlers: 12 hours
    - Three- to twelve-year-olds: 10–12 hours
    - Teens: 9–10 hours

8. **Good sleep hygiene.** This could consist of taking a bath or shower before bed to help your kid to relax, no heavy meals or large sugary drinks close to bedtime, only light snacks (bananas are particularly good). Lights should be dimmed as you get towards bedtime (think lamps rather than overhead lights) and no screens just before as the blue light of screens wakes our brains up and so prevents the usual bodily signals that say it's time to switch off and go to sleep.

9. **Screen time limits.** Research has shown the more screen time the higher the risk of your kid developing anxiety. I don't share this here to scare you but just to show the relationship and the need to not have unfettered access to screens for any of us, let alone the kids.[33]

Why is self-care so important?

The easy answer is it helps us and our kids to combat stress. A little bit of stress in our lives is actually healthy for us. A little spike in cortisol and adrenaline, both natural stress hormones, is what gets us through exams, driving tests, etc. However, too much can have a negative impact on our physical and mental health. It is important to look out for when that balance is tipped in the wrong direction.

Clear signs of stress in our kids can look like this:

- Complaining of headaches
- Appetite changes (increased or decreased)
- Stomach pain (often kids store anxiety in their stomach)
- Lethargy or lack of motivation
- Change in sleeping habits – not being able to fall asleep or not being able to get up in the morning
- Negative self-talk – for example, 'I can't, I'm no good'
- Wanting lots of noise – no quiet time (thinking time)
- Crying
- Isolating themselves

- Becoming a perfectionist
- Panic attacks
- Bouts of anxiety
- Over-worrying or thinking
- Absence of happiness, laughter or joy

Younger ones may also experience:

- Bed wetting
- Biting their nails, skin or other kids!
- Talking less or lots more than usual

Something to note: What we perceive to be stressful is not the same as what our kids may think is stressful. When asking students about what stresses them out, their answers can be anything from forgetting kit for school to being asked to do too many things at once, to homework, exams, a change of plans (whether at home or with friends) ... and the list goes on.

Most of those things wouldn't really register with most adults, so it's important that we don't diminish how they feel by saying things such as 'you don't need to worry' or 'don't be silly.' We run the risk of shutting the kids down and them internalising the stress that they are feeling. Offer them the opportunity to talk about it. 'I am here if you want to talk about it' or 'What can I do to help you? Let's take it one step at a time.'

Parent cues

Self-care is taking responsibility for ourselves. It starts with our physical body but also spreads to our emotions and mental capacity too. This can be everything from physical care such as getting enough sleep, washing hair, exercising, emotional care, taking time out to wind down, and expressing emotions and needs. What can we do to encourage self-care in kids?

1. **Practise it ourselves.** Often as parents we hold ourselves up to high standards. Role model for your kids. Let them see what you do as an act of self-care. It could be anything from taking a day off work to ordering pizza for dinner.

2. **Make a list.** Get your kids to make a list of go-to things that help them in times of stress. (See full list of examples of emotional regulation in chapter 4.)

3. **Listen to music.** I often get teens to make various playlists, one to play when they are sad and need to get it out, one for when they need more energy and one when they need to get out of a funk.

4. **Go for a walk or run.** Getting out in nature helps calm our nervous system, improves mood and blood pressure.

5. **Connect with a friend or family member**, whether this is in person or over video call. (While nothing replaces seeing people face-to-face, research shows our feeling of connection and cognition in our brains improves.)

6. **Clean your room.** This isn't just because we like it clean, it helps shift any stale energy in the room and gives them a sense of satisfaction. They deserve a nice clean room

to sleep in and it will improve their mental well-being. I often help my kids with this, when they need a reorganise or they have let it get too messy. We might sort some clothes out to give away to younger kids in the family or go to the charity shop. This also helps them feel they are doing something nice for someone else too – boosting oxytocin – their happy hormone.

7. **Technology detox.** Have designated times when no one has their device in hand. These times could be when eating together, on a Sunday morning or when watching movies together.

8. **Find what works.** Allow them to experiment with what works for them. During the teen years what that looks like might change. Exercise could change from going to the park with friends to going to the gym instead.

> 'We can't practise compassion with others if we can't treat ourselves kindly.' – Brené Brown[34]

Connection and belonging: claim your kid!

In my experience, connection is the biggest foundation that resilience is built on – and I would go further by saying a sense of belonging too. As human beings we thrive on connection – not the LinkedIn or Facebook connections, but real relationships that have a physical presence in our life. It has been well documented that infants who are fed regularly but don't receive human contact with a significant adult often won't survive. Lack of connection can have more of a detrimental effect on our health than obesity, smoking and high blood pressure. Research also highlights that when scanning children's brains, those with little to no social connection have a reduction in the growth of the left hemisphere – the part of the brain that is responsible for speech, comprehension and reading, among other things such as sequencing and logical reasoning.

Everyone – from a toddler dancing in a coffee shop in front of strangers, an older person living alone, a businessperson presenting at a conference to a teen expressing their opinion at home – just wants to be **seen and heard.**

In our young people, we can see that those who have strong connections have:

- Less anxiety
- Lower depression rates
- Stronger immunity
- Higher self-esteem and empathy
- Better emotional regulation
- Less anti-social behaviour
- A fifty percent chance of living longer!

Belonging

As kids hit puberty, everything in their DNA compels them to pull away from us as parents and identify with their peer group. It has been this way since cave times and ensures the survival of the species. That said, we need to make sure our kids know they always have a safe place to return to, where they will always belong, despite what happens with friendships.

Amelia Franck Meyer gave a TEDx talk about the human need for belonging.[35] She takes the concept of belonging one step further and says we need to feel not just that we belong but that we are 'claimed' by at least one person. It is fundamental for kids to feel safe and that they belong, for them to learn, grow and thrive.

When we don't feel like we belong we will seek connection out elsewhere, often in places or with people that might not be a positive influence. This is why gangs gain members despite often being unsafe places or going against a young person's values. It is why teens try smoking or drugs, so they can try to fit in and show they belong to their peer group.

I told the story earlier of when I was small and any news of me would reach my nanna before I could. This was my sense of being claimed. She once tackled a large and foreboding dinner lady who was force-feeding me my vegetables (my nanna was barely five foot tall). I knew then and there she would always be in my corner for good or bad and I was six-years-old. Growing up with the sense you belong to someone gives you confidence to try hard things and new experiences. I was lucky to come from a large family, I knew I always had a place, and that someone always had my back.

Parent cues

How do we foster connection and belonging for our kids?

1. **Claim them!** Make sure, without a shadow of a doubt, they know they belong to you and they have a place in the family unit. They know that whatever happens you have their back! This starts with listening to them, so they feel they can come to you with the big stuff, the difficult conversations around sex or drugs. Give them the time to unload their thoughts and feelings before jumping in with your opinion.

2. **Commit to connection.** It's not about the iPhone or the big presents and things we give them, it's about the time we spend with them. If you don't believe me, ask them what they got last Christmas or what was their best day out. You will see which is indelible in their memory. For a connection boost try the magic ten minutes activity or the daily teen challenge (both in the free resource section at the front of the book).

3. **Be mindful when talking to kids.** Life is busy and often we are multitasking, whether it's cooking, checking our phone or just being distracted through tiredness after a busy day. When our kids or teens need attention, their brain can detect if we are present, or not. Either ask them to be patient and wait while you finish what you are doing or to give you a minute while you gather yourself, then give them your FULL attention. They know if you are thinking about what you're going to make for dinner, rather than listening to their story!

4. **Model good friendship skills.** Talk about your friends and the things you do for each other, even if it's just listening to each other. Talk through appropriate problems you may have had with friends and how you solved them.

5. **Take an interest in their friendship circle.** Chat to their friends and invite them round. Whether they are in nursery or college, chat about them. Always talk with respect about their friends and try not to criticise – it won't end well. It will, however, provide opportunities to discuss the negative impact of peer pressure or boundaries with them.

6. **Encourage playdates or sleepovers.** Set them up with kids that are important to your child – everyone loves a sleepover, no matter the age.

7. **Look for who is in their connection circle.** It's not just about us as parents being their cheerleader but other adults around them. Does their rugby coach, dance teacher, school assistant, grandparent or a cool aunt also light up when they enter a room? Stay connected to these other important people in your kid's life, because when your young person is having a hard time, they will be a valuable source to lift them back up.

8. **Arrange time with wider family or friends.** We meet up with friends who live hundreds of miles from us a couple of times a year. We have been friends for years. They have a girl and boy older than my eldest and one the same age as my youngest. It is

a time for us to connect and catch up with genuine interest in each other. The older kids take a real interest – they chat about school, college, TikTok, friendships and lots of other stuff. It is great because it gives a different perspective to the ones they hear from us and their usual friendship circles. It also models adult friendships for them. This meet-up is filled with lots of laughs and it's glorious to listen to.

9. **The friendship journey.** Teach kids about the fluidity of friendships. A wise friend of mine once spoke about friendship like being on a train journey. Some get on at the same time as you, they may stay on for a few stops, others will get on and off quite quickly, others may last the journey all the way to the end. Don't be afraid if friendships don't last the whole journey. We learn lots from friendships, particularly about ourselves. Sometimes people may come into our lives to teach us that we need to put boundaries in place. Explaining to kids not all friendships are built to last helps them not to take it personally.

Connection before direction

In chapter four, I spent some time reminding (or teaching!) you that we are the ones in the room with the fully-formed brain, the prefrontal cortex which makes our logical decisions. Remember, when kids flip their lid, they haven't got access to this part of the brain. This is where you are going to use connection to your advantage!

Dr Jody Carrington talks about 'connection before direction'.[36] This means connecting with our kids before we talk to them about what just happened to make them flip their lid. Does it mean they get away with bad behaviour? Absolutely not. But as we know, they can't hear us when they can't access those parts of the brain that help make good choices and we need to calm them down quickly. We do this by connecting, letting them know we are in their corner, lighting up when you see them walk in the room and walking with them through their emotions. In essence, we are co-regulating.

This often goes against what we have been taught about consequences and rewards in the behaviour model very much present in traditional parenting books. But I am here to tell you that kids want to do well, they want to please those they have that connection to. Connecting with your kids when they do something wrong or make a bad choice **first**, before you talk through what happened, will not only strengthen your relationship with them but it will also give them the skills and insight they need for their future, especially when they don't have you around.

'The more healthy relationships a child has, the more likely they will be to recover from trauma and thrive. Relationships are the agents of change and the most powerful therapy is human love.' – Dr Bruce Parry[37]

I started this section talking about how connections are the foundations of resilience – they nurture our basic needs as humans, help us navigate the social aspects of the world around us and combat stress that life may throw our way. Connections also boost our purpose and community contribution by honing skills such as empathy and compassion. If we teach our kids the importance of strong connections, they are more likely to show vulnerability with those connections and have happier and healthier relationships that support their very resilience.

Conclusion
Walking with them – one step at a time

I want to finish with a story of a girl who against the odds built her wall of resilience and made it. Let's call her Zoe.

Real-life example

In Zoe's family, her dad left when she was young and he now had another family with young children. She lived at home with her brother and mum. She went to a large high school and had a small group of friends. Zoe developed an eating disorder which consumed her every thought and she suffered academically. Zoe came to see me after being referred by a concerned teacher. She was a gentle soul who had wrestled with self-harm previously but what I noticed first was her eyes. She had the most beautiful smile – but it didn't quite reach her eyes. As we began to get to know each other and unpick her story, I discovered her wicked sense of humour and a strong streak of creativity. As her story began to un-ravel, it was clear that she felt abandoned – not just by her dad, who was now busy with his new young family, but also by her mum who was the sole financial provider for the family. Her mum worked long hours and had no extended family around her for support. She often came home late and ate in front of the TV, leaving the kids to eat in their rooms. Specialised support was sought for the medical aspects of Zoe's eating disorder and I was there to help with the emotional support while she was in school. We began very gently with both Zoe and her mum, recognising the lack of support within the community for both of them. We began by giving Zoe a network of teaching and pastoral support within the school; she also ate lunch with a teacher every day and, with her permission, every staff member was aware of her situation. Not one of them spoke about it but it meant that when she walked down the corridor, staff would smile and chat to her, asking about her day or next lesson. Zoe was being seen! In our sessions together we worked on her self-image, confidence and her responsibilities, including self-care. Zoe wanted to change the way she felt about herself and worked hard in sessions, not shying away from the challenges therapy brought up for her. Work with her mum included getting her support, establishing boundaries and acknowledging the eating disorder – and also education around how it worked and how best she could support her daughter. She didn't feel dissimilar to Zoe, being the one left with the responsibility of two children, both financially and emotionally.

Coupled with a fantastic medical programme and the progress she was making in sessions, Zoe felt able to put herself forward to join a peer mentoring programme. She was a firm favourite with the younger pupils looking for help with friendship issues. She then began recruiting more of her year group to join as mentors, and she would lead them in assemblies and training sessions. She did this, all the while working hard on eating patterns and her therapy appointments. Today, Zoe is in her last year of university, studying Psychology. She has a boyfriend and is absolutely thriving. She has a fantastic relationship with her mum and brother, both of whom, as you can imagine, are so proud of her. Zoe has had other issues in her life since, but she has the determination, support and resilience to deal with what life throws at her. To build Zoe's resilience was a village effort, with teachers, specialists, family and friends all around her showing her she was seen, heard and that she belonged.

It is easy to get overwhelmed with the responsibility and weight of getting parenting right. To build our kids' resilience we must look at the factors such as how to boost their confidence, to teach them responsibility and empathy, to encourage connections to friends, family and their community, to give them opportunities to contribute and to be able to find their purpose. We want to encourage gratitude for the small things in life, as well as the big. However, let's not forget, you won't be starting from scratch with all of these. And on that note:

I want to remind you about two things.
1. Our job as parents is to walk them home, guiding them on the way with all our imperfections, through this thing we call life.
2. We, as parents, only have to get it right thirty percent of the time for our kids to turn out OK. So, leave the parent guilt at the door. You are doing a good job; you wouldn't be reading this book if you didn't care.

So, take a look at where your child is lacking in resilience, check which components might need a boost and begin to implement the easy and practical strategies you have already read about. It may be as simple as signing them up to an after-school class, arranging to see extended family more, or raising their confidence levels higher with small challenges.

Our most important job comes simply by showing up.

Dr Dan Siegel and Dr Tina Payne Bryson write about this in their book, *The Power of Showing Up:*

'One of the very best predictors for how any child turns out – in terms of happiness, social and emotional development, leadership skills, meaningful relationships, and even academic and career success – is whether they developed security from having at least one person who showed up for them.'[38]

I would go one step further and say yes, one hundred percent show up for your kids with all your imperfections in tow, but also be the one who **lights up when you see them.** Kids will often mirror our moods, so when they greet you at the school gate or walk in the door from a tough day at school, light up and have a big smile ready to listen to their day. You will literally light up twelve different parts of their brain and flood them with love hormones, confirming you are always in their corner. And on those days when you're not feeling the big smile, the listening ear – tell them, model for them, and allow them to give you the empathy you might need.

So, go! Deepen that connection with your kids, let them know you have their back, build their wall of resilience and let's be that village and future-proof them together.

Acknowledgements

A BIG THANK YOU GOES to Erin Chamberlain, Editor extraordinaire. You have been an absolute brick through the whole process and I couldn't have done it without you. Thank you for your kind words, unwavering support and polish.

Sally Graphics (Tyson) – thank you for your patience and interpretation of scribbles and garbled voice messages.

To the Lady Writers – I love you not just for the late night chats, fabulous food and face masks but most of all steadfast confidence in me – you're next!

To the hubby – Dave Kelly. Thank you for believing in me and picking up the slack when I run off for yet another writing weekend – I love you!

Auntie Pat – thank you for always being supportive and excited no matter what I am up to! Love you x

Dr Jody Carrington – for showing the way, leading therapists home and knowing we can do our work with authenticity and without the stick up our arse – thank you!

To Zoe, you know who you are – thank you for teaching me as much as I guided you! Know you will always be seen and heard here. Take care of you x

ASHLEY COSTELLO IS A PSYCHOTHERAPIST, TEDx speaker, researcher and now published author. Born in South Africa, raised in Manchester, lived in Abu Dhabi, and now settled in the lush countryside of Cheshire with hubby Dave, two kids and two cats. When not working with clients or delivering training, Ashley likes to swim in open water and cook for her friends and family. She hopes to finish building her house this year with said hubby.

Check out the latest from The Resilient Kid via the following links:

www.theresilientkid.co.uk
https://www.facebook.com/resilientkiduk
https://www.instagram.com/resilientkid/
https://www.theresilientacademy.co.uk
ashley@theresilientkid.co.uk

Drop me a line and let me know how you got on with the book!

Endnotes

1   African proverb, source unknown.

2   NHS Digital, 'Mental Health of Children and Young People in England, 2020', October 2020, https://digital.nhs.uk/data-and-information/publications/statistical/mental-health-of-children-and-young-people-in-england/2020-wave-1-follow-up.

3   NHS Digital, 'Mental Health of Children and Young People in England, 2020'.

4   James S House, Karl R Landis and Debra Umberson, 'Social Relationships and Health', *Science Magazine* vol 241, issue 4865 (1988), pp.540–545, https://science.sciencemag.org/ content/241/4865/540.

5   Ram Dass and Mirabai Bush, *Walking Each Other Home: Conversations on Loving and Dying* (New Mexico: Sounds True Inc, 2022).

6   Maya Angelou, https://mayaangelou.com/.

7   Esther Mesman, Annabel Vreeker and Manon Hillegers, 'Resilience and mental health in children and adolescents: an update of the recent literature and future directions', *Current Opinion in Psychiatry* vol 34, issue 6 (2021), pp.586–592.

8   Dan Siegel, 'Minding the Brain', *Pyschalive*, 2010, https://www.psychalive.org/minding-the-brain-by-danielsiegel-m-d-2/.

9   NHS Digital, 'Mental Health of Children and Young People in England, 2020'.

10 Definition of 'resilience', *Concise Oxford English Dictionary* 12th Edition (Oxford: Oxford University Press, 2011).

11 Thomas Boyce, *The Orchid and the Dandelion: Why Sensitive People Struggle* (London: Bluebird: 2019).

12 Siegel, 'Minding the Brain'.

13 Erica L Kenney , Michael W Long , Angie L Cradock and Steven L Gortmaker , 'Prevalence of Inadequate Hydration Among US Children and Disparities by Gender and Race/Ethnicity: National Health and Nutrition Examination Survey, 2009–2012', *American Journal of Public Health* vol 105, issue 8 (2015).

14 M Di Simplicio, R Massey-Chase, P J Cowen, and C J Harmer, 'Oxytocin enhances processing of positive versus negative emotional information in healthy male volunteers', *Journal of Psychopharmacology* vol 23, issue 3 (2009), doi.org/10.1177/0269881108095705.

15 B F Skinner, 'Operant Behavior' in W K Honig (Ed.), *Operant Behavior: Areas of Research and Application* (New York: Appleton-Century-Crofts, 1966), pp.12–32.

16 Jess Lair, *I Ain't Much, Baby – But I'm All I've Got* (Bantam Doubleday Dell, 1972).

17 Clayton R Cook, Aria Fiat, Madeline Larson et al, 'Positive Greetings at the Door: Evaluation of a Low-Cost, High-Yield Proactive Classroom Management Strategy', *Journal of Positive Behavior Interventions* vol 20, issue 3 (2018), pp.149–159.

18 Judith Locke, *The Bonsai Child* (Queensland: Confident and Capable: 2015).

19 Karen Young, 'Hey Sigmund: Building courage in kids and teens', https://www.heysigmund.com.

20 Wendy Rose Gould, 'How to get better at admitting you're wrong', 6 June 2019, *NBC News*, https://www.nbcnews.com/better/ lifestyle/ how-get-better-admitting-you-re-wrongncna1003356.

21 Henry D Thoreau, *Walden* (Boston: Ticknor and Fields, 1854).

22 Brené Brown, 'The Power of Vulnerability', TEDx Houston, 2010, https://www.ted.com/talks/brene_brown_the_power_of_vulnerability?utm_campaign=tedspread&utm_medium=referral&utm_source=tedcomshare.

23 R J R Blair, 'The amygdala and ventromedial prefrontal cortex in mortality and psychopathology', *Trends in Cognitive Sciences* vol 11, issue 9 (2007), pp.387–392.

24 Virginia E Strum, Howard J Rosen, Stephen Allison, Bruce L Miller and Robert W Levenson, 'Self-conscious emotion deficits in frontotemporal lobar degeneration', *Brain* vol 129 (2006), pp.2508–2516.

25 Definition of 'guilt', *Cambridge Dictionary, https://dictionary.cambridge.org/dictionary/english/guilt*.

26 Definition of 'shame', *Concise Oxford English Dictionary* 12th edition (Oxford: Oxford University Press, 2011).

27 B Amsterdam, 'Mirror self-image reactions before age two', *Developmental Psychobiology* vol 5, issue 4 (1972), pp.297-305, doi: 10.1002/dev.420050403.

28 Hiromi Taniguchi and Gul Aldikacti Marshall, 'The Effects of Social Trust and Institutional Trust on Formal Volunteering and Charitable Giving in Japan', *Voluntas* vol 25 (2014), pp.150–175, doi.org/10.1007/s11266-012-9328-3.

29 Amy McCready, *The Me, Me, Me Epidemic: A step-by-step guide to raising capable grateful kids in an over-entitled world* (Tarcher, 2015).

30 Jinho Kim and Kerem Morgül, 'Long-term consequences of youth volunteering: Voluntary versus involuntary service', *Social Science Research* vol 67 (2017) pp.160–175.

31 Michelle Mitchell, *Everyday Resilience* (Big Sky Publishing, 2021).

32 Brené Brown, *Daring Greatley: How the courage to be vulnerable transforms the way we live, love parent and lead* (Penguin Life, 2015).

33 Jean M Twenge and W Keith Campbell, 'Associations between screen time and lower psychological well-being among children and adolescents: Evidence from a population-based study', *Preventive Medicine Reports* vol 12 (2018) pp.271–283, doi: 10.1016/j.pmedr.2018.10.003.

34 Brené Brown, *Rising Strong* (Vermilion, 2015).

35 Amelia Franck Meyer, 'The Human Need for Belonging', TEDx Minneapolis, 2016, https://youtu.be/0nlcpVAAZ0k.

36 Jody Carrington, *Kids these days: A game lane for (Re)Connecting with those we teach, lead & love* (IMpress, 2020).

37 Bruce Parry, *The Boy who was raised as a dog, and other stories from a child psychiatrist's notebook: what traumatized children can teach us about loss, love and healing* 3rd Edition (Basic Books, 2017).

38 Dan Siegel and Tina Payne Bryson, *The Power of Showing Up* (Scribe UK, 2020).

Index

Printed in Great Britain
by Amazon